Discovering
Speyside

FRANCIS THOMPSON

JOHN DONALD PUBLISHERS LTD
EDINBURGH

ISBN 085976 230 0

Phototypesetting by Newtext Composition Ltd., Glasgow.
Printed in Great Britain by Martin's of Berwick Ltd.

Contents

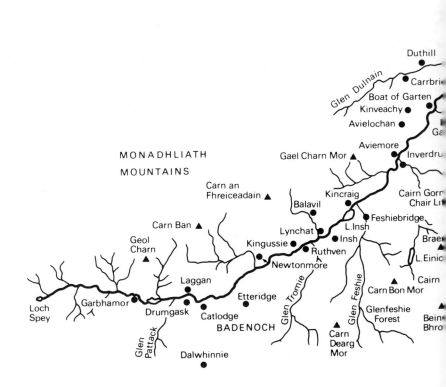

Duthill
Carrbri
Glen Dulnain
Boat of Garten
Kinveachy
Avielochan

MONADHLIATH
MOUNTAINS

Gael Charn Mor ▲

Aviemore
Inverdru
Ga

Carn an
Fhreiceadain ▲

Kincraig
Balavil

Cairn Gorr
Chair Li

Carn Ban ▲

Lynchat
Kingussie
Ruthven

L.Insh
Feshiebridge

Geol
Charn ▲

Newtonmore

Insh

Brae

L.Einic

Cairn

Laggan
Etteridge

Carn Bon Mor

Loch
Spey

Garbhamor
Drumgask

Glen Tromie
Glen Feshie

Glenfeshie
Forest

Bein
Bhro

Catlodge
BADENOCH

Glen Pattack

Carn
Dearg
Mor

Dalwhinnie

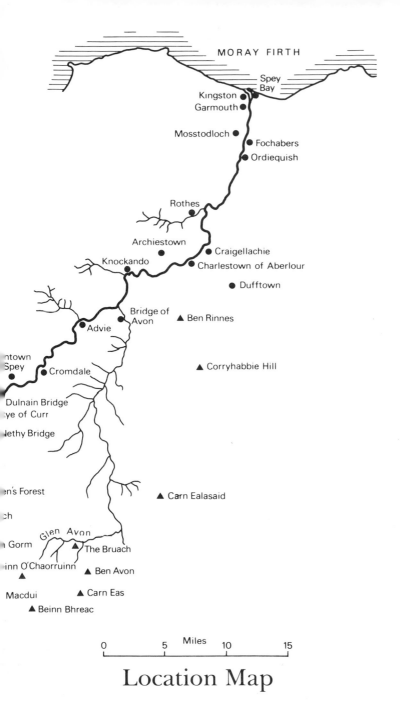

MORAY FIRTH

Spey
Bay

Kingston ●
Garmouth ●

Mosstodloch ●

● Fochabers
● Ordiequish

Rothes ●

Archiestown ●
● Craigellachie
Knockando ● ● Charlestown of Aberlour

● Dufftown

Bridge of
Avon ▲ Ben Rinnes
Advie ●

▲ Corryhabbie Hill

ntown
Spey
● Cromdale

Dulnain Bridge
ye of Curr

lethy Bridge

en's Forest

ch

▲ Carn Ealasaid

Gorm   Glen Avon
▲ The Bruach
inn O'Chaorruinn
▲   ▲ Ben Avon

Macdui   ▲ Carn Eas
▲ Beinn Bhreac

0   5   Miles   10   15

Location Map

Introduction

Were it not for the fact that a small loch in the Monadhliath Mountains gives perpetual birth to an equally small but brawling river there would be no theme to this book of discovery. But because the youngster is fostered by other rivers on its way to the sea, the River Spey quickly reaches its majority as it flows into the Moray Firth. Again, had the Spey simply meandered through low-level land to no purpose it would be just another river.

But there is much more to the Spey. It has had an impact on Scottish and Highland history, on Speyside's human settlements through the centuries and provided the incentive for exploitation both in the past and in our own times. Add to this the presence of the Cairngorm Mountains, among the highest in Britain, and we find that Speyside begins to hold the attention of the visitor. And if we further mention the fact that Scotland's production of the golden liquid, whisky, is concentrated on Speyside, that also serves to heighten one's sense of anticipation.

Over the past two decades or so, Speyside has become synonymous with sports and pleasure pursuits and certainly many visitors come to Speyside with one activity in mind. But to do so exclusively would be to deny the pleasure of discovering those aspects of an area which can broaden the mind and increase one's understanding of what makes a place 'tick'. There are, however, no magnificent palaces and castles to visit, to taste at second hand the ostentation of the aristocrat. Castles there are, to be sure, but they are now silent witnesses to a turbulent past written in the pages of Highland history. There are no great monuments to famous sons, like the once President of the United States, Ulysses Grant, whose forebears came from Speyside. There is, in fact, no obvious boasting – achievements are worn lightly.

But that is in the nature of the character of Speyside. Rather, it is the environment which dominates today and certainly it was the environment in the past which governed the life and living of the Speyside folk. Glimpses of the impact of the

The Cairngorms as seen from above Aviemore. The River Spey curves its way along the floor of the Strath in one of its more leisurely moods. Though this picture was taken in the height of summer, there are still residual patches of snow which the sun has failed to dislodge. *(Courtesy Scottish Tourist Board)*

environment as it was can be seen, for example, in the Highland Folk Museum in Kingussie, or in the Fochabers Museum. Clan history is viewed in the Clan Macpherson Museum in Newtonmore. Churchyards are silent but powerful witnesses to the unsung history of the folk who once lived and worked under the shadow of the Cairngorms.

At the Kincraig Wildlife Park one can see the living evidence of the range of animals, many now extinct, which roamed the old Caledonian Forest when it covered much of the Highlands of Scotland. And the Speyside forests themselves tell their own story of cutting, burning and regeneration.

Speyside is very much an outdoor place with virtually unrestricted access to scenic wonders and vistas which take the breath away, landscapes which contain a whole kaleidoscope of interest: from intimate forest walks to the more challenging heights of the Cairngorm peaks where, in the rarefied air, the mind takes on a kind of pleasant feyness.

This book takes the reader of its first chapter into the

Self-reliance was the keynote to Highland living in times past. Here a staged scene in the Folk Museum at Kingussie, shows a typical room set aside for the weaving of cloth. But the stages before the yarn was ready for the loom had to be completed. These included washing and dyeing the wool, carding into 'rolags', spinning and then warping the threads into the pattern which was to be woven. The loom is an old type of wooden design, one of a very few which are now in existence. *(Courtesy of Scottish Tourist Board)*

physical environment of Speyside to set the scene. Chapter 2 describes the wildlife in which the area abounds, from the imported herd of reindeer (an echo of Scotland's past) to the bird that has now become the symbol of Speyside: the fish-eating osprey. The next four chapters are devoted to the route of the River Spey, as it journeys through the human settlements which have looked on the river as both enemy and friend.

Because the River Spey would not be the same without its tributaries, Chapter 7 describes the impact of these waters, many of which sustain the Speyside whisky distilling industry which produces Scotland's 'liquid gold' reserves. In Chapter 8 the mountains of the Cairngorms are rightly given the prominence they deserve, for it is because of them that Speyside now rivals many of the holiday centres of Europe,

A scene in the still house at Rothes distillery. Two craft skills are involved here. The distillation process which proceeds away from prying eyes with only the stillman to check that quality is being maintained. The other skill is the final product of the coppersmith's craftsmanship: the shaping of the stills to a time-worn formula which must never change if the distillery's product is to remain consistent. *(Courtesy Scottish Tourist Board)*

added to which were it not for the snow facilities available on their slopes the future Winter Olympic stars of Britain would have to go abroad for their routine training.

The last two chapters are concerned with the manner in which the resources of Speyside have been exploited for both pleasure and profit, the latter aspect taking the reader into a seventeenth-century world of financial speculation and the consequent destruction of much of the Old Caledonian forest. Whisky is not ignored, being a product of Speyside which more than keeps Britain's balance of trade in reasonable health, to say nothing of keeping aficionados of the 'dram' at peace with the troubles of the world.

One last word. Over the past decade there has been a real and significant improvement in the facilities being offered to the visitor, from comfortable accommodation to meals which remain in the memory of the taste buds for long enough. Information leaflets are now thick on the ground, as Speysiders realise that visitors need to do more than wander around the area aimlessly.

Discovering any area needs time and a slow savouring of the ingredients which all combine, in some alchemic way, to make up what is called Speyside, Strathspey, or the Spey Valley. Not all of what the area has to offer will appeal to all visitors. Some will be single-minded: 'Hey-ho, the Skiing!' But even skiers must pause for a break and wonder about the workings of Nature whose craftsmanship produced the Cairngorms. Dedicated bird-watchers must recognise that all wildlife react with each other and the environment and so find other avenues of interest. Those who have a penchant for trout or salmon fishing on the Spey and its tributaries have ample time for reflection as they wait for a 'rise' to consider the importance of these waters to the folk of Speyside in past times. And those who come to Speyside just to get away from it all, will find plenty to see and do, thus adding an extra dimension of interest to their stay.

This book, then, is a bit of a temptress who whets the curiosity and satisfies 'the need to know'. If it does that, then the reader will share with the author the double bonus of education and pleasure which he derived while this book was being written.

CHAPTER 1

The Sculpted Landscape

Few rivers in the British Isles have a course, from source to the sea, which runs through one of the most magnificent landscapes in Europe. In its journey of less than 100 miles, the River Spey makes its way, at times in a great hurry and at others almost lazily, from the desolation of the Monadhliath Mountains past the massive plateau of the Cairngorms and then through low country until it reaches the flat lands of the Moray Firth coast. Its course takes in an astonishing variety of landforms, all of which add a significant dimension of interest to the visitor who intends to sojourn in Strathspey and to those who pass through the Spey Valley to go farther north into the Highlands.

For the early part of its course, the Spey is accompanied by the peaks of the Monadhliath Mountains. This range of peaks is slightly lower than the Cairngorms, but has similarly stepped surfaces extending from the Spey to Loch Ness and is littered with peat bogs and glacial debris, all bearing witness to the meeting point of ice sheets from the Ness and Spey valleys. Like the Cairngorms, the Monadhliaths are based almost wholly on that hard impervious rock: granite. The peaks lie along the watershed between the Rivers Findhorn and Spey and consist, for the most part, of broad level surfaces with a dominant level of about 1000 feet. There are large dumps of glacial material, with some remarkable overflow channels which cut deep into the basic rock. One example can be seen in the Slochd to the north-west of Carrbridge.

Compared to the popularity of the Cairngorms, the Monadhliath area is seldom visited, with only the Corrieyairack Pass sensing the press of human feet as hill-walkers make the trek from Fort Augustus to Speyside. Otherwise, the area to the west of the Spey is an ageless region of Nature in the raw, a true expanse of wild desolation as yet unbreached by the demand for tourist access.

Wade's Road, Corrieyairack Pass. *(Photograph: Hamish Brown)*

Their very accessibility has, on the other hand, made the peaks of the Cairngorms something of a Mecca for a variety of visitors, from those who prefer the low-level walks among the forests, to those who 'want to climb a mountain' and the élite: those experienced mountaineers who challenge the sheer walls of difficult corries.

Of course, what we see today as the Cairngorms is the result of land-forming processes which were going on well before the Ice Age, around 10,000 years ago. The original sharp-cut, faceted peaks have been smoothed over, with massive weighty glaciers acting as sandpaper to produce more rounded forms which, though they may lack dramatic features, still give much pleasure to the eye. But something of the original landscape still survives. Precipitous cliffs cut into gently-flowing slopes and deep gullies and gorges, jagged ridges and high profiled tors all betray the fact that the ancient slow-moving glaciers did not quite manage to level everything in their path.

The work of the glaciers is still spectacular, however, with the cliffed valleys which bite deeply into the mountain massifs. The steep-walled Lairig Ghru, for instance, is impressive from any

stance or viewpoint. In fact it is such a natural feature of the
Cairngorms that it acts as a flight line for migrating birds. In
the western Cairngorms, Loch Avon, Glen Einich and Glen
Giusachan display the result of glaciers which once poured
over steep head-walls.

The glaciers also left vast expanses of low-lying ground
consisting of sand, rubble and rock debris, now seen in the
hillocky nature of the ground covered by poor vegetation and
peat.

While the mountainous areas of Strathspey are impressive
enough, the lower reaches of the River Spey offer interesting
evidence of the past and present entirely different scenery.
One particular feature at the mouth of the Spey is the low
undulating nature of the land, to say nothing of its fertility.
This is due to another rock-base. While the Cairngorms are
based on hard granite, towards the Moray Firth the base rock is
Old Red Sandstone, which occurs on the eastern seaboard of
the Highlands from Caithness down to the Moray Firth. This
rock is a sedimentary product. Whereas igneous rocks are
produced by internal processes within the earth, sedimentary
rocks are formed by processes which have been active on the
earth's surface. The surface of the land is being continually
attacked by weathering and erosion caused by rain, wind and
moving ice. These agents, when they are assisted by chemical
decay from percolating waters, break up even the toughest of
rock and produce rock waste. This is then carried, mainly by
rivers, to be deposited as a sediment at river mouths, in lochs
and in the sea. The gradual accumulation, which can be many
miles thick, is an excellent base for fertile soil. The sedimentary
rock also contains an important secret: fossils, the remains of
animals or plants, usually the hardest parts of the organisms,
which tell us so much about life in the earth's formative eras.

The area concerned here is fairly low-lying. Most of the
higher hills are around 2400 feet. These include the ridge of the
Cromdale Hills which separate the River Spey from the River
Findhorn. The prominent granite peak of Ben Rinnes, to the
west of Glen Rinnes, stands, at 2775 feet, as a reminder, with its
attendant sgurrs, of its association with the rock of the
Cairngorms. Northwards from Ben Rinnes, the land falls away
quickly in hills below 1600 feet to the Moray Firth coastline. A

The Moray coast at the mouth of the Spey. The hill is the Bin of Cullen. *(Photograph: Hamish Brown)*

great depth of river- and ice-carried material covers lower Moray from the western boundaries of the present district. An indication of the thickness of these huge deposits, which were dumped against the edge of the huge ice-sheet which is sometimes known as the Spey Glacier, can be seen at Binn Hill near Garmouth, which is composed of some 230 feet of these materials. These deposits have in their time been extensively re-shaped by marine action at the higher sea levels of late- and post-glacial eras, as well as that of the present day, producing the complex terrace features which merge with those of the lower reaches of the Spey, and the River Findhorn some miles to the west.

The great age of Strathspey is indicated by the river valleys in relation to the rivers they contain. The solid geology of the district has controlled the drainage system. The largest system comprises the Rivers Spey, Avon, Livet, Dullan Water and the Fiddich, with the Spey being the longest river. For its valley to have attained the proportions of the present day is an indication that the river must have, during its history, cut away all soft rocks between the Monadhliaths to reach the true bed

9

of hard rock. The River Avon, however, is no less interesting because it has actually beheaded the River Don which flows to the east coast of Aberdeenshire. It is thought that the Avon at one time cut back along a strike or outcrop to capture the head waters at the Don, the older of the two rivers, which drained eastwards at Inchory.

The Spey, too, has its history of diversion. Northwards at Craigellachie the Spey is diverted by a fault which runs from Dufftown to the Glen of Rothes. The weakened rocks at this fault zone also offered an easier alternative for the River Fiddich and the Dullan Water, which at one time flowed into the Isla but are now tributaries of the River Spey.

When the Spey arrives at its middle reaches it finds itself in wide-bottomed valleys with little gradient and by the time it passes into Moray District it is actively cutting down into the basic rock and taking pot-luck with its direction. This latter idiosyncrasy is seen in the way the river cuts new runs in its attempt to reach the sea, for, on this low-lying ground, it tends to meander as it flows over the unconsolidated deposit material which forms the coastal plain.

Thus, changes in the Strathspey landscape still occur. One of the major agencies in this respect is the flooding of the Spey Valley. For the extent of this area, Strathspey has a most efficient drainage system, associated with a huge catchment area. The result has been a history of repeated floodings, and often changes in the flow directions of rivers, and the Spey itself in particular. It was this fact that caused the loss of previously reclaimed carse land, notably along the Spey between Kincraig and Ruthven.

This area is saturated with chemically-rich water and, as on the floor of a main valley, has produced an extensive peat-forming sedge marsh, of the kind known as 'fen' rather than bog. Along the alluvial flood-plain of the Spey Valley below Kingussie is one of the largest fens now remaining in the British Isles which rivals those of the Norfolk Broads.

This huge swampland ends at Loch Insh and stretches for three miles long by one mile wide on either side of the Spey. In the past there have been attempts at drainage and some of the drier areas have in fact been reclaimed to produce pasture land; but now the old drains are mostly choked by vegetation

The Old Caledonian Forest – predominantly old Scots Pine but often with birch and juniper as here. *(Photograph: Hamish Brown)*

and the area often floods in winter. The construction of artificial banks on the Spey and the railway embankments along the northern side have probably contributed to impeded drainage within the Insh fens. This is in fact an ancient swampland, with peat up to eighteen feet deep in one place. At Kincraig, the Spey broadens out to form the large and fairly deep Loch Insh.

Other changes in the landscape occur as the result of natural events, such as the formation of gulleys. This is the most spectacular sign of erosion, both geological and accelerated. These often follow exceptionally heavy rainfalls, when excessive water produces mud-flows on the grassy slopes of the schist hills, to lay bare the subsoil, with its uncompacted sands, gravels and glacial debris, originally covered over with thin layers of peaty soil and thin vegetation growth.

An example of the way river banks erode can be seen on the River Nethy, where the water has undercut the face of the river terrace, resulting in debris slides. Other examples include the areas on hillsides where trees have been felled and sheep allowed to graze. The roots of the former trees are exposed, indicating a measure of the soil that has already been lost. Road-building in the Cairngorms has also created large areas of denuded and unsightly peat and stony debris which, with a really heavy cloud-burst, could start a landslide.

Just such a situation occurred in August 1978 when a mountain burn burst its banks and left more than one hundred people stranded on Cairngorm overnight. Torrential rain caused the Ault Mhor burn to become so swollen with water that an avalanche started which took boulders and rock debris downstream until they became lodged under the single-arch Coronation Bridge. Unable to pass under the bridge, the water flooded onto the roadside to a depth of three feet. This road leads up to the Cairngorm ski-lift and was busy with tourist traffic. Although many tourists had left the mountainside in response to police 'flashflood' warnings, many cars were left stranded with their occupants, the latter being rescued within twenty-four hours of their ordeal. In this instance, as was the case in an earlier similar incident, there were no casualties. But the incident underlined the fact that the possibility of sudden flooding taking away parts of the road is ever present and could in the future take cars and their occupants down the hillside.

The appearance of Man in the Spey Valley was the result of the potential the area offered for exploitation, as seen in the possibilities for agriculture, themselves related to the soils found in the valley and on the hill slopes. Much of the soils of the higher-level areas is still in the process of formation. Some are less than 10,000 years old, the result of the rocks being broken down by weathering and chemical activity and mixing in with the clays, sands and gravels; they are also fertilised by the decay of vegetation. The soils tend to be mineral in content on the higher slopes, but become more organic in nature where

Grantown on Spey. *(Photograph: Hamish Brown)*

humus has been allowed to build up successive layers.

Nearer the Moray coast, the softer rocks of the Old Red Sandstone have accelerated the soil-making processes and produced high degrees of fertility as evidenced at the present time in the type of vegetation and crops now being grown.

One major feature of the vegetation cover in the area is the Old Caledonian Forest, which once covered most of the Highlands and remnants of which are still seen in places in the valley of the Spey. The prehistoric colonisation of Scotland began the long tale of forest clearance which has continued until modern times. Then the gradual extension of cultivation caused more forest areas to disappear, a process not reversed until the eighteenth century, which time saw a new phase of planting and which heralded the beginning of a reafforestation and conservation.

The indigenous tree cover can be seen everywhere. The pine and birch have a long-standing association with the ancient forest cover; the latter are to be found on all poorer thin soils where pine and oak grew formerly, and can be seen growing at altitudes up to the 2000 feet level. Remnants of oakwood forest, of well-drained sands and gravel soils are found in glens and valleys. The pine in our present-day climate is not able to regenerate itself once it is cut or burnt. This fact was recognised by the middle of the fifteenth century when legislation was introduced by the Scots Parliament to slow down or halt the destruction of the country's forests. Populated lowlands and straths were being denuded of trees and the process of deforestation was spreading into the remoter upland areas.

However, there are many stands of pine which are the descendants of the trees of the Old Caledonian Forest, some trees being as much as 200 years old. The Scots pine is very much a tree of the granite and is able to flourish on poor soils resting on a layer of glacial drift. On Speyside, the pine wood stretches in a discontinuous belt from Glenfeshie in the south-west to Nethybridge in the north and includes the famous forests of Invereshie, Inshriach, Rothiemurchus, Glenmore and Abernethy.

Human settlements have naturally occurred on the valley floor where the soil is richest and at natural nodes, for example where the mountain valleys descend on to the plains and at the convergence of river systems. Settlements also grew up round a fort or castle, built in areas of comparative agricultural wealth, where the land could be farmed easily and livestock raised with little difficulty.

Later settlements were established because of economic activity or, as in the case of Grantown on Spey, founded in 1765, the need to create a town to act as a focal point for a small but important area which had potential for growth. Other settlements grew up with the advent of the railway, with their economies based on tourism. Yet other towns and villages were created to accommodate people who had been cleared from their former lands and because of their potential to act as a workforce on estates. Some towns were set up around a religious establishment; others around a religion of a different kind: whisky distilleries. Thus, the settlements in Strathspey, generally following the course of the River Spey, present a wide range of origins, with the underlying common theme of providing a satisfying environment for life and living as offered by the forces of nature in times past.

The River Spey has always been one of Nature's unruly

Loch Insh – the view from the Sailing School.
(Photograph: Hamish Brown)

children, often giving pleasure but equally able to change its character to cause havoc to the settlements along its banks. Particularly in the lower reaches of the river, in Badenoch (derived from Gaelic: Drowned Place) the river was always known for its frequent flooding, especially on the haughs or low grounds which lie between Kingussie and Loch Insh.

There are many records of the Spey floods, some recalling memorable incidents. Draining, as it does, some 1300 square miles of mountainous territory, and a flow of some 98 miles, with contributions of mountain waters from numerous tributaries, the volume of water making its way to Speymouth is always considerable. Thus, in times of excessive rains or massive falls of snow in the process of thawing, the river system becomes incapable of carrying the water in normal channels and flooding results.

Such a combination of factors went to cause the great flooding of the Spey Valley in 1829. The first few days of August of that year saw a deluge pouring from the skies. In the neighbourhood of Belleville and Invereshie the river widened into a tempestuous sheet of water five miles long by one mile wide. In Glenfeshie the inhabitants had to flee for their lives before a wall of water. One sea captain from Coulnakyle, in the Abernethy district, who had in his years weathered many a

15

rough gale, saw his 200 acres flooded so that when the waters subsided, only fifty were worth cultivating. He reported: 'I am satisfied that I could have sailed a fifty-gun ship from Boat of Bellifurth to Boat of Garten, a distance of seven or eight miles'. The River Dulnain destroyed the Bridge of Curr, a single span arch of 65 feet, in its intent to reach lower levels. In the Abernethy district alone, the floods destroyed 13 bridges, three sawmills, three mealmills and a great many houses, together with the loss of many acres of growing crops. At Inchroy, the River Avon rose to a height of 23 feet. Great landslips occurred; whole farms were swept out of existence and the waters actually created new channels for themselves. The Plain of Rothes was completely covered and carried 'a heterogeneous collection of spinning wheels, chairs, cradles, tables, beds, chests of drawers and every manner of cottage furniture and farming utensils, all indication in a pathetic way of the ravages of the swollen rivers'.

The streets in the village of Rothes became rivers in themselves, pouring water into the houses. The Bridge of Spey at Fochabers was destroyed with the weight of water pressing against its supporting pillars. It had four arches, two of 95 ft and two of 75 ft span each. The water rose to a level of 17 feet above normal and cracked the structure, throwing some people into the flood waters when the bridge finally collapsed.

Loch Insh, normally three miles long and one mile across, had its water level raised to about eight feet. An account of the great flood reads: 'The River Feshie . . . swept vast stones and heavy trees along with it, roaring tremendously . . . The crops in Glenfeshie were annihilated. The romantic old bridge at Inverfeshie is of two arches, the larger being 22 feet above the river in its ordinary state, yet the flood was three feet above the keystone. Several sheep were found alive on the tops of the trees at the foot of the garden of the inn at Aviemore. At the mouth of the river more scenes of devastation were witnessed by onlookers. In Garmouth and its vicinity about fifteen houses were destroyed opposite to the sawmill of Garmouth, where the width of the inundation was fully a mile . . . at Kingston Port, the water rose over 13 feet'.

So great was the body of water rushing into the sea at Garmouth that no tide could enter the mouth of the Spey. As far as the eye could see, the plain was covered with water, and the beach, the harbour, and along the sweep of the bay was studded with stranded vessels and covered with one huge heap of wreck from both river and ocean – composed of immense quantities of wood, dead animals and furniture of all kinds.

The 1829 flooding stands unparalleled in a history of flooding in the Highlands. A lesser calamity occurred in 1892, in midwinter. In this instance, the most dramatic piece of destruction was the loss of a section of the Highland Railway immediately below Belleville, halfway between Kingussie and Kincraig stations. The line was carried on an embankment some ten feet high. The last train to pass to the south just managed to cross over the breached section of the embankment with the water level being so high as to almost extinguish the engine firebox. Another train actually left Kingussie for Inverness but was stopped in time by the driver sighting danger signals placed on the rails by surfacemen. If this had not happened, the train and its passengers would have taken a death dive.

A dramatic account by a witness of the 1892 flood survives: 'From Fochabers to the mouth of the Spey at Garmouth, the river presented in miniature the appearance of an inland sea. The land here is almost level, and the great body of water, as soon as it passed the confined area between the bed rocks west of Fochabers, spread out in both directions, completely covering the extensive area of whins and undergrowth. On to the sea the vast volume of water swept, carrying everything before it, cutting out for itself new channels, filling up old ones, and submerging all objects within its reach. Not since the flood of 1829 was such a vast area of the surrounding country under flood in this district, and not, probably, since that date had the river presented so picturesque and awe-inspiring a sight. Onward the river rolled with an impetuous fury, the waves dashing and breaking as in a storm at sea, ever and anon striking at the massive supports of the bridge, which, standing firm as a rock, resisted the aggression with apparent ease. It was a grand sight to watch from the gigantic structure the seething, eddying mass of water rushing underneath with the roar of a mighty cataract, angry in mood, as it were, because science had rendered the viaduct invincible against its terrible power'.

The River Spey still presents a constant danger from flooding, though measures have been taken to ensure that any damage caused by flooding is minimised. In 1977 there was seen the completion of the new mouth cut for the Spey at Kingston. This new mouth was cut to reduce the risk of future flooding and to prevent further erosion and the build-up of shingle in the area. The cutting was made about a half-mile to the east of the former river mouth. Thus the unruly Spey is being tamed. One of the most vulnerable parts of the Spey river banks is that great extent of meadow land below Kingussie. In the past this tract became a temporary lake sometimes over six miles in length which at times threatened the stability of the railway line running close by. Dykes were erected in the most vulnerable places, but the underlying surface of water still presents a problem at times, and the land is often wet and marshy. Loch Insh is merely a remnant of the old lake which at one time extended all the way from Kingussie.

What the visitor to Speyside sees today is merely the result of many changes in the landscape, some recent, others going back into the mists of time. Some of these changes have been imperceptible. Others are of more recent origin, with the evidence apparent to the careful observant eye. The changes are all, however, part of the history of a fascinating area in which the master is the turbulent River Spey.

CHAPTER 2

Feather, Fur and Scale

The land on both sides of the River Spey, as it makes its way from its source, through the drowned lands of Badenoch, past the Cairngorms and into the lush lands of the Moray Firth, offers a range of habitats for flora and fauna which is, in many respects, quite unique in the British Isles, if not in Europe. To say that about Speyside is not simply a sweeping statement but an undoubted fact which has emerged from decades of close study by naturalists with both broad and specialist interests. Certainly, the area encompassing the Spey Valley offers such a wide spectrum of species for close study and casual observation that it is not surprising that fears are now being expressed for the safety and continued existence of nature in its raw states, particularly as more demands for tourist developments come on to the drawing boards. Indeed, what was called 'wilderness' a few decades ago is now becoming accessible to large numbers of people who, rightly, wish to see the grandeur of the wild.

If one hand-crafted and magnificent species sums up the natural gifts of Speyside, it is the osprey, an example both of man's attitude to wildlife, on the one hand heedless of the consequences and, on the other, his change of heart and attitude in the light of new knowledge and the appreciation of the fact that all living things contribute to the balance of a scheme of things in which man is but a complementary element. It is a sign of sanity that many people now involved in the conservation of wildlife, even though they might offer only token support in a subscription to a conservation organisation, perhaps a decade or so ago would not have done much else than show or share passive concern.

It was the nineteenth-century visionary and mystic poet, Francis Thompson, who wrote: 'Thou cans't not stir a flower without troubling of a star'. That statement, far in advance of its time, contains the idea that all living things on earth share the common experience of life and that the fate of one entity can impinge on the consciousness of others. While the gift of

19

mental association with other persons and living things might be too deep-sunk in the subconscious of many, there are not a few who still display this gift in such experiences as telephathy precognition. But for most of us it is sufficient that we be aware of the instrinsic values of wildlife.

Human societies in close contact with nature have always been the most aware of the need to conserve, and to live within an environment circumscribed by local pressures and opportunities. One of the perfect examples of this is seen in the approach to life of the American Indian, as written in 1835 by Chief Seathl of the Swamish tribe in a letter to the President of the United States: 'How can you buy or sell the sky – the warmth of the land? The idea is strange to us. Every shining pine needle, every sandy shore, every mist in the dark woods, every clearing and humming insect is holy in the memory and experience of my people . . . The air is precious to the red man. For all things share the same breath – the beasts, the trees, man . . . The white man must treat the beasts of this land as his brothers. I am a savage and do not understand any other way. I have seen a thousand rotting buffaloes on the prairie, left by the white man who shot them from a passing train. I am a savage and do not understand . . . What is man without the beasts? If all the beasts were gone, man would die from loneliness of spirit, for whatever happens to man. All things are connected . . .'

Such simple concern expressed so long ago has now been reinforced by those who today see the need to conserve what nature has to offer. Particularly in the Cairngorms area, battle lines are often drawn up between developers and conservationists, with the latter being accused of interfering with progress. These accusations are countered by the question: 'At what cost?'

The osprey has rightly been chosen as a symbol of Speyside, for its come-back in recent years almost underlines the increased awareness of the very species which reduced its number to the point of extinction many years ago. The story of the osprey, how it was shot out of Highland existence by 1902 and its return in 1954 is told in a later chapter. But nothing comes easy. Operation Osprey at Loch Garten has had three seasons of disappointment which left a question mark over one

A ptarmigan. *(Photograph: David Gowans)*

of Scotland's most popular tourist attractions. The hide, overlooking the artificial eyrie created by the Royal Society for the Protection of Birds, has attracted more than 1.3 million visitors since 1959.

The last hatching at the Loch Garten site was in 1984. Then in 1985 the male bird at the nest damaged a wing and the female had to take over the role of food provider. The eggs were placed in an incubator but only two hatched. One chick died and the other had to be fostered out to another eyrie elsewhere in Scotland. In 1986 a female returned to the artificial eyrie which had to be attached to the 60-ft high nesting tree to replace the portion which had been cut down by vandals. But the 1986 eggs chilled and failed to incubate.

In 1987 the nesting pair unfortunately broke their eggs. Those at Loch Garten were deeply disappointed. However, in 1988 three chicks were hatched in the first week of June and were amply provided for by the male bird. In July the chicks were brought down from the nest and ringed, and then replaced with the expectation that they would fly off in early

August. Hopefully they will return to Loch Garten and continue the gradual build-up of the species on Speyside.

If the osprey is the symbol of Speyside, then the golden eagle must surely be the symbol of the wilderness which the remoter parts of Speyside represent. Between the Monadhliath Mountains and the Cairngorms, including Deeside, there is a small, but rather static, population of these magnificent birds, which can often be seen soaring like moving punctuation marks against the skyline. But whatever their beauty, they are still the targets for stalkers and gamekeepers. The bird is protected under the Protection of Birds Act, 1954, but is often killed illegally in remote hill country and its nests robbed. A pair of breeding eagles requires between 4000 and 18,000 acres to sustain them: one reason why the bird, if seen, is usually a solitary winger. The main importance of the Cairngorm eagles is that they represent a reservoir of reasonable stock, uncontaminated by organo-chlorine pesticides which are often the fate of eagles in other areas, and they could be used to stock new ground or repopulate lost territories.

The snow bunting is one of the rarest of Scottish birds. In the last 100 years or so, hunters have found fewer than fifty nests with eggs in them in the Cairngorms. In historic times only a few pairs have been known to nest on these arctic slopes. These birds, more common in Greenland and Iceland and in Scandinavia, are actually at their southernmost limit for breeding, which accounts to some extent for their rarity. The cock bird has a black mantle, white wings and ebony primaries, and a sighting is a red letter day in any bird-watcher's diary.

Other hill birds in Speyside include the dotterel, which is now making a come-back to recolonise a few of the lower hills, and the ptarmigan, usually found wherever crowberry or blueberry are abundant (on ground with boulders and screes). One must climb to see these birds, at least to 2000 feet. The ptarmigan was a popular 'shoot' in Victorian times, when it was fashionable to go out on wholesale-slaughter expeditions. Nowadays it is the honest and innocent tourist who represents the greatest danger to the ptarmigan, by damaging or destroying vegetation on the hills with fragile areas. Even so, the species manages to keep its numbers up, even on the disturbed habitats near the ski-lifts of Coire Cas and on Cairnwell.

Loch Garten. *(Photograph: Hamish Brown)*

The dotterel adds a charming vignette to the Cairngorms scene above the 3000ft levels, with its deep chocolate crown, white cheeks and eye-stripes which meet at the nape; a broad white crescent separates the brown of the upper and lower chest and flank. It was first noted hereabouts in 1769, when Thomas Pennant was touring the Highlands. Less than twenty years later it was the target of the extrovert sportsman, Colonel Thornton, who killed one bird with a tiercel and shot another.

In recent times the dotterel has begun to breed on the lower slopes, and this represents a danger to the population, for the birds are quite tame and are easy prey and playthings for dogs not kept on the leash. Both crows and peregrine falcons are not averse to taking dotterels; but the population, low as it is, seems to survive to add its contribution to the excitement of a sighting.

These species might be said to be included in the crown jewels of Speyside bird life. But they are by no means all that can be seen in the area. Both in the relict boreal forest and on the arctic-alpine tops other species can be observed, like the snowy owl frequently seen on the Ben Macdhui-Cairngorm plateau over the last few years. Other species include snow

23

buntings, dunlins, golden plovers, peregrine falcons, snipe, black grouse, goosanders, to name but a very few from the rich catalogue of bird species in the area. Not to be ignored are the migrating northern birds such as wild geese, redwings, fieldfares, some wild duck, brambling, whimbrel, Temminck's stint . . . the list is seemingly endless. This rich pageant occurs simply because Speyside covers so many different habitats.

Animals are more readily seen and spotted in Speyside. Perhaps one of the most interesting is a foreigner, yet was once a native of Scotland: the reindeer. Caithness, in the north of Scotland, is supposed to have been the last place in the country where the species survived until the twelfth century. There is a tradition that the Jarls of Orkney, in the tenth century, were in the habit of crossing the Pentland Firth to hunt the reindeer in the wilds of Caithness. The species was more than familiar to ancient man. A reindeer appears on a carved stone of the early Christian period, found at Grantown on Spey, indicating that the recently introduced animal was no stranger to Speyside and the Cairngorms.

Attempts to re-introduce the reindeer to the Highlands were made in the eighteenth century, when the Duke of Atholl released about a dozen into the Atholl Forest, and then in 1820 when the Earl of Fife introduced some reindeer on Mar, on the east side of the Cairngorms; but none of these animals survived. In 1954 some mountain and forest reindeer were transported from Swedish Lapland to low ground in Glenmore but they failed to thrive. Later the British Reindeer Company, under the guidance of the late Mikel Utsi, a Lapp from northern Sweden, settled a small herd inside a fenced enclosure on forest marsh near Moor Bing. After that the herd was moved to an area south of Loch Morlich, enclosing old pine forest and windswept moorland. The object of the experiment was to find out whether the animals could be satisfactorily established on a commercial basis, without any addition to their staple diet of reindeer moss. In summer the animals now roam on the Ben Macdhui plateau and Carn Lochain. The present herd numbers over 100, all Scottish-born.

Both roe deer and red deer are a common sight in the Speyside area, in Rothiemurchus, for example. The red deer,

A golden eagle on its nest. *(Photograph: David Gowans)*

however, are mainly confined to the glen bottoms, in old woods and on hillsides below 2000 feet. Severe winters tend to take their toll of the red deer and the animals are often seen in poor and distressed condition.

Other animals of Speyside and its high slopes include mountain hare, common shrew, weasel and mink, the latter escaped from captivity where they were bred for furs in Glen Livet until 1965. Since then increasing numbers have been killed along the rivers but they are still spreading fast. They are cruel and vicious animals, now that the populations are in a feral state.

One animal which never fails to excite interest is the wild goat. Although feral goats disappeared from the Cairngorms earlier this century, a group now lives on the rocks near Carrbridge. The original animals existed in what is now Glenmore National Park. But one wild winter, an avalanche struck the herd and completely destroyed it, with no survivors. The present population in parts of Speyside came to some prominence a decade or so back when a row flared up in the Press over the shooting of wild goats on a Speyside estate. The goats, in fact, do present something of a problem. They breed rapidly and, in the absence of natural predators, can quickly destroy all kinds of plant life and all too soon find themselves in a goat-created desert. The herd on Creagdhu, between Newtonmore and Laggan, are reasonably tame.

The mammal fauna which once existed in the Highlands were very rich indeed. Many species once native to the region are now extinct. The improvement of the climate after the last glaciation in Scotland extinguished such animals as the mammoth, woolly rhinoceros, musk ox, cave bear, giant fallow, arctic fox and the lemming. The red deer of Pleistocene times were replaced by the smaller forms of the present day. The elk, reindeer, wild cat, bison, brown bear, wolf and beaver survived into historic times. The bison and wild cattle were probably the first to disappear in the early Iron Age. The bear may well have existed until the tenth century; the reindeer and elk a little longer. And there are reports of beavers in Inverness-shire in the sixteenth century, and wild boars until the early seventeenth century.

The European bear was once a common animal in the Old Caledonian Forest. Bishop Leslie tells us that this great woodland was once 'refertissima', full of them. Camden, another writer of old, says: 'This Athole is a country fruitful enough, having wood vallies, where once the Caledonian Forest (dreadful for its dark intricate windings and for its dens of bears) extend itself far and near in these parts'. Camden also quotes Plutarch in saying that Scottish bears were transported to Rome '. . . where they held them in great admiration'. During the Roman occupation of Britain, Caledonian bears were well known in Rome for their exceptional beauty and size, and they were prized as one of the animals able to provide bloody spectacles in the Colosseum and other Roman amphitheatres. A number of Gaelic-based placenames in the Highlands indicate that the bear was commonly known.

The wild boar was one of the oldest animals in the British Isles and is the one which has the earliest mention in history. The Gordon family, which eventually came to own much of Speyside, was given the right to sport three boars' heads on its banners: the result of an ancestor who, about 1057, had killed a fierce boar in the Forest of Huntly.

The wolf, too, was once common in Scotland, so much so that it was necessary to erect refuges for the safety of travellers overtaken by nightfall, for fear of an attack by the animal. These refuges were called Spitals, a name which occurs, for example, in the Spittal of Glenshee, on the Devil's Elbow road from Blairgowrie to Braemar. One of the last wolves to be killed in Scotland was a beast which breathed its last at the hands of a stalker to The Mackintosh, named MacQueen, who dispatched the animal near the River Findhorn in 1743.

The fate of many of the now-extinct animals was often a result of their direct links with man who, for various reasons, found himself unable to tolerate their presence. Often regarded as vermin, fit for nothing but sport, they were hunted and killed in great numbers. Many recorded instances tell of organised hunts which ended in wholesale slaughter. While it can be argued that the wolf, for instance, was a real danger to the human species in Scotland, it is perhaps a cause for regret that a true native of the Highland wilderness had to be weighed in the balance and found wanting, thereby removing an interesting specimen from the natural museum which the Highlands have often offered extinct, rare and threatened species. But that is an argument which could carry on into the wee sma' hours over a good malt whisky from Speyside.

Some small but significant act of reparation for what happened in the past is seen at Kincraig, at the Highland Wildlife Park, where many of the animals once indigenous to the Spey Valley and the Cairngorms are kept in a free-roaming environment, and where, too, are to be seen some examples, brought from other places in the world, of now-extinct Highland animals.

Viewing these, one tends to appreciate all the more the efforts of those who are now trying to bring back some of the things which man has lost without pangs of regret, but which somehow still remain on his conscience.

The River Spey and its tributaries, and Speyside's lochs, have always been noted for their fish populations, and salmon and trout in particular. Access to these waters has, however, always been in dispute and recent legal battles have produced gains and concessions as well as losses.

Salmon fishing was a communal sport ('one for the pot') until about 1850; the fish provided food for the farm labourer and it was caught by lights, nets and pronged forks. The later years of last century saw the 'sporting' types flock into the Highlands for some diversion and the salmon in particular became the guarded property of estate owners and a status sport for the wealthy. Fishing by forks became illegal in 1868. The local people then reverted to poaching, using nets, gaffs (hooks snatched through the water) and the illegal bait of salmon eggs. These methods are still used.

To the devoted and enthusiastic angler, the Spey in particular offers excellent sport, though in recent years the sea stock of salmon has been so depleted by factory fishing outside British territorial sea limits that the fish is not so plentiful now as it was. At the time of writing an Irish trawler skipper was arrested at sea with 460 illegally-caught salmon on board.

The Atlantic salmon swim up river from the sea from October onwards. In some mild winters, when there are periods of high water, they can be found as far up the Spey as Aviemore; in most years, however, they tend to stay in the lower reaches nearer the mouth, which is why beats on the river there have the best early fishing. The fish spawn in October and November in gravel redds or nests, usually in the larger tributaries and in small streams. The fish are good climbers and salmon have been known to spawn well past Laggan on the Spey, and have also been seen at heights of over 1800 feet above sea level, above the Tromie, the Avon and the Feshie rivers.

After spawning, a large number of fish tend to die, but some, particularly females, manage to get back downstream again to reach the sea to return, in another autumn, to spawn again.

Although the sea trout are often smaller than salmon, some fish weighing over 20 lb have been caught in the rivers of the Cairngorms. Most sea trout enter fresh water in summer and make for the tributaries which drain the middle and lower reaches of the Spey's watershed. Unlike the salmon, the sea trout tend to feed in fresh waters when they reach adult stage.

Brown trout, unlike the migratory sea trout, are widespread in lochs and streams up to 2500 feet. In some waters, lack of proper feeding tends to make the fish rather thin. For those who want to try their hand at catching fish, the fish-farm at

A dotterel in the hills of the Cairngorms. *(Photograph: David Gowans).*

Inverdruie offers the best opportunity.

Char and pike can be found in Speyside waters, the former more associated with Loch Insh. The pike were introduced into Scotland a long time ago and now are resident in the main valleys of the Spey, in Loch Insh and Loch an Eilean. In 1786 Colonel Thornton, a keen sportsman, described some huge pike in the waters in Badenoch.

As part of the activities offered on Speyside, a number of angling courses are available to introduce newcomers to the sport and to help veterans to improve their fishing and casting techniques. In all the courses the emphasis is on casting proficiency rather than the taking of fish. It should be mentioned that fishing beats on rivers in Speyside can be costly, especially for those wishing to catch salmon. It is, sadly, nowadays, a sport for the very rich.

CHAPTER 3

The Corrieyairack to Newtonmore

The River Spey begins its 98-mile journey north to the Moray Firth in Loch Spey, which lies between the Forests of Corrieyairack and Braeroy. It is not a big loch by normal standards, yet it is mother to the second longest river in Scotland. Loch Spey is some 1143 feet above sea level and is on the border marches between Badenoch and Lochaber. These areas are so redolent of Highland history that they seem to have passed on its atmosphere to the river which, among few such in Scotland, has created for itself a niche in the affairs of the country at large.

The Spey makes a respectable 'fall' in its first few miles, being fed by the tumbling waters of over thirty small tributaries before it reaches the flat lands around Kingussie. Then, collecting more water from other tributary rivers, it flows along, sometimes quietly, at times boisterously, until the mouth is reached at Kingston on the Moray Firth, where even the strength of the sea tides fails to force sea water upstream for much more than half a mile.

Loch Spey is fed from streams mainly from the slopes of Creag a' Bhanain to give the Spey the bulk of water needed to maintain the Spey's reputation of being the most rapid of all rivers for its size in Britain. Its average fall from Loch Spey to its mouth is 11½ feet per mile, compared with, for example, under two feet for the River Thames. In addition, unlike most rivers which tend to flow gently into the sea, the Spey actually increases its pace in its journey from source to mouth. This creates the inevitable problem of flooding when both sea and river waters meet, particularly when the Spey is in flood and a good gale is blowing from the north-east.

The Spey meets up with human history less than five miles from its source when it merges with the waters of Allt Yairack, flowing from the Corrieyairack Pass, at Melgarve. There are many passes in Scotland, those orchestrated depressions in a geological symphony which play so many important roles in the

Kingussie in the distance with the River Spey in one of its quieter moods. One can easily imagine the low banks on the left being flooded when the River becomes swollen with winter rain and melting snow from the mountains. *(Courtesy Scottish Tourist Board)*

history of human settlements. Some are famous: Glencoe and Killiecrankie conjure up a vivid pageantry with little effort. Some others are, however, equally deserving of fame, but are often kept obscure from the public eye by their very inaccessibility.

The Corrieyairack Pass carries a road built by General Wade in 1732, running from Cullachy, just south of Fort Augustus on Loch Ness, to Dalwhinnie, at the head of another Pass, the Drumochter. Much of the route of this road follows the young River Spey as it flows towards Newtonmore. The road was built primarily to allow the easy shift of Government troops between the barracks then being built in the Highlands. The period which followed the 1715 Jacobite Rising was one of extreme unrest in the Highlands. The Disarming Act of 1719 served only to increase the feeling of bitterness among the Highland clans. Lord Lovat, for one, among other well-known and prominent Highland chiefs, insisted in a 'memorial' (or letter) that the Government take steps to stop further disaffection and disloyalty.

In response to these requests, Major-General Wade was instructed to make his way to the Highlands and report on Lord Lovat's memorial. He arrived in the north in July 1724 to begin work, and by December he had finished his survey and received a commission as Commander-in-Chief of the military forces in North Britain. His report included a number of recommendations for 'reducing the Highlands to obedience'. He stated that money would be required for 'the mending of roads between garrisons and barracks for better communication of His Majesty's Troops'. For once, a Government responded with alacrity and by the end of 1725 Wade had begun the construction of his great military highway through the Great Glen, from Fort William to Inverness. This was followed by the building of the road southwards from Inverness to Dunkeld, in Perthshire. Then, in 1731, he began the building of a road from Fort Augustus over the Corrieyairack to Dalwhinnie and Dalnacardoch, and on to Aberfeldy and Crieff. These constituted the three main lines of communication built by Wade between 1725 and 1733, a period of eight years during which, with some minor connections, he engineered a total of 250 miles of roadway. In 1740 Wade was relieved of his command and died in 1748, at the good old age of 75. He is buried in Westminster Abbey.

Of all his roads, the Corrieyairack was the toughest task. Some 500 men were employed on the project. The rough work was carried out by military parties under the command of their

The view from Cope's Turn looking towards the Corrieyairack Pass.
(Photograph: Hamish Brown)

own officers, with extra pay being allowed for the extreme
conditions they encountered. Then the masons and skilled men
moved in to construct the actual road. The most difficult part
of the route was the road up to the south face of the
Corrieyairack, which required a series of seventeen traverses,
later reduced to thirteen.

Robert Chambers, of the Edinburgh publishing family,
described the traverses: '. . . each of which leads the traveller
but a small way forward in the actual course of his journey. A
stone buttress some ten to fifteen feet in height retains each
traverse on its outward side; while a drain or water-course was
constructed on the inward side'. Another impressive feature
was the double-arched bridge spanning the River Spey at
Garvamore, named St George's Bridge, after King George II.
It is a handsome structure of two arches, each of 40-ft span,
joining the centre pier which stands on solid load-bearing rock
in the middle of the river.

The road through the Pass runs for 22 miles and was
completed in about six months. The statistics indicate that it
was finished at the rate of one yard per man per day, a feat

which is impressive even in terms of the sophisticated techniques available to road-builders in these modern times. The spring of 1732 saw the road in full use for wheeled vehicles and the transport of troops and artillery. Wade himself drove over it with his officers in a carriage drawn by six horses. It is said that his appearance on the summit (2922 feet above sea level before it falls steeply through the watershed of the River Tarff) caused no end of consternation among the Highland hill folk who witnessed the incident.

At first, Wade's roads were resented, not unnaturally. They represented easy access to the hitherto inaccessible tracts of land owned by Highland chiefs who claimed that the coming of strangers among them threatened to '... destroy or weaken that attachment of their vassals, which is so necessary for them to support and preserve'.

If the new roads were intolerable, the bridges were even more so. The chiefs held the view that the provision of bridges across rivers and turbulent streams would make the people effeminate, and incapable of crossing other rivers without artificial aids. Indeed, progress has always had a hard time of it to make itself acceptable!

In time the road through the Pass became accepted by travellers, drovers and others. The drovers, however, tended to criticise the road, claiming that the hard core wore down the feet of the cattle on their way to the trysts at Crieff and Falkirk. Often the cattle had to be specially shod to protect them on their long treks. The year 1880 saw the last of the herds of horses brought over the Pass to the Falkirk tryst; cattle were driven over it until 1896 and sheep until 1899.

Over the years many travellers have provided descriptions of their experiences in the Corrieyairack: 'It was certainly cold enough for my greatcoat; but I became neither torpid nor frozen. I discharged my plough horses . . . When I came to the beginning of the zig-zag, the sun began to shine; and to the south-west, above the rest of the mountain ocean's waves, I saw Ben Nivis, which I distinguished from the other mountains, it being rendered conspicuous by the sun shining upon its white patches of snow. At the commencement of the zig-zag I got out of the carriage and walked down at my leisure; amusing myself by picking up curious stones and pebbles in the channels made

Garva Bridge, the finest Wade bridge on the Corrieyairack route.
(Photograph: Hamish Brown)

by the torrents, which cross the road at every five or ten yards. Round the base of the mountain, at some distance from the zig-zag, is a stream, into which other torrents dash; leaving behind them broad channels of smooth stones, washed from the higher parts. The road is so cut up by these torrents, from the top of the zig-zag to the entrance of the plain, that for four or five miles scarcely ten yards can be found free of them; which is, indeed, sufficient to pull a light carriage to pieces. Allen led the horses, and the wheels being dragged, he came quietly and safely to the bottom of that extraordinary pass . . .'

Perhaps the most famous traverse of the Corrieyairack was made by the troops of the Forty-five Rising under Bonnie Prince Charlie.

In charge of the Government's troops was General Sir John Cope. Hearing rumours in July 1745 that the Prince had landed somewhere in the Highlands, he advised the Secretary for Scotland, Lord Tweeddale, that the various Highland forts should be supplied with arms and ammunition. But the Government was nervous and ordered Cope to take an army into the Highlands to nip any rebellion in the bud. Cope himself was just as apprehensive, for he would be taking his troops into terrain with which the Highlanders were all too familiar, and they would have all the advantages.

He decided to march to Fort Augustus, over the Corrieyairack Pass, a route which would have brought him into direct confrontation with the Jacobite army. Indeed, when Prince Charles heard the news that Cope was encamped at Garbhamore he was thrilled: 'Before I take off these broguews I shall engage with Mr. Cope!' But Cope was beset with problems. His troops were in no condition to face a fierce and bloody battle, particularly when he was informed that the Highlanders were entrenched in the Pass and that he would not be able to break through to Fort Augustus – alive, let alone wounded.

After thinking long and hard, he decided to head north for Inverness; after all, his orders were indeed to head north, so he considered that if he did so he would not be criticised. So Cope retreated from his encampment on the banks of the Spey and made for Inverness. Not far from Dalcholly House, a little to the west of Laggan, there is a small group of trees known locally as Cope's Turn, marking the place where he abandoned his intended advance westwards to Fort Augustus. His retreat allowed the Jacobite army to make its leisurely way south. Cope was later to make his own mark on the pages of Scotland's history with his defeat at Prestonpans when he became the butt of the most famous rebel song of the whole campaign: 'Hey, Johnnie Cope, are ye waukin yet?'

Although now much deteriorated, the road through Corrieyairack is still passable. One needs good weather, some stamina and ability and good walking gear, for this is rough country. All the bridges survive in part or entirely. Where they are not usable, crossing is not too difficult. The four or so miles from Melgarve to the summit (over 2500 feet) is rough walking. But the experience of tackling the zig-zags or traverses is both tiring and rewarding.

From Melgarve the Spey hurries on over a rocky channel at Garva Bridge, Wade's magnificent two-arched structure, well buttressed to take the power of the river's rushing waters, particularly when the Spey is in flood. It is a compliment to Wade's engineers that it has stood the test for nearly 250 years.

Calum Piobair Memorial Cairn. *(Photograph: Hamish Brown)*

Nearby is Garbhamore (Garvamore on the map) where the remains of the Kingshouse stand. It was built by Wade to shelter troops as they trekked from one side of Scotland to the other. Prince Charles slept here on his march southwards from Fort Augustus. Two of the old box-beds in the building now repose in the West Highland Museum at Fort William.

From Garbhamore the Spey flows eastwards into an expanse of water dammed at one end by the Spey dam. A little to the south is the Black Craig on top of which sits the ancient fort of Dun-da-Laimh (the Fort of the Two Hands). It occupies a superb position on the tip of a long promontory ridge which divides the main valley from Strathmashie. The flanks of the ridge fall steeply from the summit to the Spey's flood plain nearly 600 feet below. The approach to the fort is only reasonably easy along the spine from the south-west. The structure conforms to the shape of the crag and measures some 460 ft by 260 ft within a wall which, as it hugs the uneven contours of the rocky outcrop, varies in width from 13 ft to 23 ft.

In some places the faces are exposed to a height of up to 9ft, revealing that the wall is built of great numbers of rather small coursed stones. The fort is reckoned to be one of the most perfect relics of an ancient stronghold of the Pictish era in the country. An old iron smelt was discovered near the summit of the Dun, with remains of ashes which showed evidence of heat far greater than can usually be obtained in a blacksmith's forge. It is something which has raised interesting speculation among archaeologists. But the answer may well be simply that the forge was constantly in use making iron weapons for a large fighting force.

Laggan village lies in a perfect setting and is in a strategic position commanding the crossing of the Spey at Laggan Bridge. To the south of the bridge, before the road turns off to the left towards Cat Lodge, there are the remains of Gaskalone Church, partly demolished when the local parishes were united. At Cat Lodge, on General Wade's road to Dalwhinnie, one can see the stone cats on the gate posts. There is a local belief that these figures must not be stroked: a reflection on the Macpherson motto: 'Touch not the cat bot a glove'.

A hundred yards or so along the road may be seen the stone cairn erected in 1960 to the memory of Calum Piobair (Macpherson) who 'preserved and taught the piobaireachd of the MacCrimmons'. Calum was piper to old Cluny Macpherson and died in 1898.

Back along the road from Laggan Bridge to Newtonmore a large stand of trees on the left hides Cluny Castle dating from the nineteenth century. The original building was the home of clan chief Cluny Macpherson, and was destroyed in the Forty-five. It was replaced by an elegant country house of superb proportions based on an Adam design. The direct line of the Macpherson chiefs ended in 1943 and the house and its historic contents were put up for sale. Fortunately some of the contents were saved by the newly-formed Clan Macpherson Association. Queen Victoria visited this area in the 1850s with Prince Albert and was sufficiently impressed to consider purchasing Cluny as her Highland home. But the inclement weather put her off and Balmoral was bought instead.

Old Cluny Macpherson looms large in the history of the Forty-five. For his part in the Rising he was made a fugitive and hid in a cave in the steep and rocky face of Creag Dubh

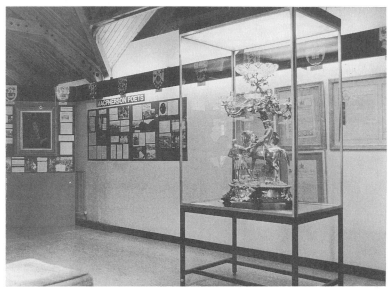

Clan Macpherson Museum. Newtonmore. In the cabinet is a large
ornamental candelabrum for a dining table.
(Photograph: Hamish Brown)

rising 2350 feet above the Spey. Macpherson hid here for eight
years, safe and sound, even though a reward of £1000 was
offered for information leading to his capture. But his
clansmen kept their secret until he shifted to France in 1754.
'Creag Dubh' is also the battle cry of the Macphersons.

Just south of where the River Truim meets the waters of the
Spey is Invernahavon, where a famous clan fight took place in
1370. The cause of the battle was the refusal of the Camerons
of Lochaber to pay rent to the Mackintoshes of Clan Chattan
for certain lands which the latter held in Lochaber. Not
unnaturally, the Mackintoshes decided that if the cash was not
forthcoming they would take their rents in kind, in the form of
cattle. So they organised a raiding party to collect, somewhat
forcibly, what was due to them. The Camerons took umbrage
at this and chased the Mackintoshes, with the Davidsons,
another Badenoch clan, back to Invernahavon. There the
Mackintoshes appealed for help from the Macphersons,
another prominent member of the Clan Chattan federation.
They agreed, but only on condition that they were given their

traditional right of holding the right flank in battle. But in the event they were allotted an inferior position, which so infuriated them that they withdrew to a hill on the north side of the Spey and sat down to watch the Davidsons and the Mackintoshes getting short shrift from the Camerons.

Appeals fell on deaf ears, until the Mackintosh chief decided to taunt them into action. He called his bard to compose a satire on the Macphersons. This was too much and the Macphersons flew down from their perches to attack the Camerons just as the latter were on the point of winning the battle and beginning to head for Lochaber. Caught unawares, the Camerons suffered heavy losses, including a number of Cameron chiefs.

To the north of Creag Dubh, at the junction of the A86, from Spean Bridge in Lochaber and the A9 main roadway from Perth to Inverness, stands Newtonmore.

The origins of the village are obscure but it is supposed that the first permanent settlers were connected with the droving trade. The low arable ground in the vicinity of the golf course is where the cattle, after being brought over the Corrieyairack Pass from Lochness-side, were herded together before being taken to the market at Pitmain, near Kingussie.

Newtonmore's main attraction is the Clan Macpherson Museum, established just after the Second World War. Many of the clan mementoes have been preserved including the broken remains of the fiddle of James Macpherson, whose name still lives on in Scottish folk music in the tune 'Macpherson's Rant'.

James Macpherson was a freebooter in the seventeenth century. Born into an illegitimate branch of the Macphersons of Invereshie, his mother was a gipsy, or tinker. He was brought up in his father's house until the latter died, when the boy was taken over by his mother who taught him the habits and ideals of her wandering tribe. James turned out to be uncommonly intelligent and displayed a number of talents, including the playing of the violin. In his youth he became the leader of a wandering party of freebooters who became noted for their Robin Hood customs of taking from the rich and giving to the poor. As a result, despite their many misdeeds, they were a popular bunch of characters among the common folk who, on more than one occasion, assisted their escape from custody.

But eventually the determined hand of the law caught up with James and he was arrested at a market in Keith and taken to Banff Jail in November 1700 to await trial along with three of his companions. The trial, such as it was, has its place in Scottish legal history as being the last ever to be held under the old laws of Heritable Jurisdiction. Under these laws the local lairds had the power of 'pit and gallows' and most trials usually ended with the death sentence. This is what happened at James Macpherson's trial; he and his companions were found guilty of various charges and sentenced to be hanged. The sentence, however, was regarded as being too harsh; banishment was the more usual penalty for robbery in Scotland. An appeal was lodged and the Strathspey community waited anxiously for the outcome.

But the Banff authorities were determined that Macpherson should die and so contrived that his hanging should take place before the appointed hour. Tradition has it that the hands of the town clock were moved forward one hour so that the hanging could be carried out before any reprieve might arrive. At the gallows Macpherson took his parting from this life lightly and defiantly. He asked for his violin and played the famous tune of 'Macpherson's Rant':

There's some cam' here tae see me hanged
And some tae buy my fiddle;
But lang e'er I shall part wi' her
I'll brak her i' the middle.

He tak the fiddle intae his haun
He brak it ower a stane.
"Nae ither haun shall gar her sing
When I am deid an gane!"

Sae rantinly, sae wantonly,
Sae dauntonly gaed he —
He played a tune and he danced it roun
Aneath the gallows tree.

When he had finished he offered the instrument to anyone in the watching crowd. But there were no takers. By accepting it they feared the gesture might be interpreted as a degree of friendship towards him and might bring reprisals afterwards.

Macpherson was saddened by the rejection of his offer and in a final gesture he broke the violin across his knee and threw the pieces among the crowd. The bits were gathered up and later passed into the hands of Cluny, chief of the Clan Macpherson, eventually to find a last poignant resting place in the Newtonmore Museum.

The ballad celebrating the incident has a number of versions, one being composed by Robert Burns. The tune to which it is sung is supposed to be that played by Macpherson himself. To add a touch of romance to the story, it is said that just after Macpherson was hanged, a messenger arrived in Banff with his reprieve.

Among other exhibits in the Museum are a letter to Prince Charles from his father, the green banner of the Clan Macpherson, and a *pièce de résistance:* a massive silver épergne (a centre piece for a dining table) which depicts an incident in the life of Cluny Macpherson after the Battle of Culloden. The Museum is open from May to September and admission is free.

Each year the Clan gathers at Newtonmore for a Rally and the Highland Games which are held on the first Saturday in August.

Just outside Newtonmore is Banchor Cemetery, known as Cladh Brighde. This resting place has an interesting niche in Scotland's legal history. It is but a generation or so since Gaelic was the everyday language of the area. Today it is spoken by very few. Yet, in all of Speyside, there is one visible piece of evidence that Gaelic was a vital factor in the life of the community hereabouts. This is a signpost in Gaelic pointing the way to St Bride's burial ground. For many centuries it was used by the folk of Newtonmore until, in 1875, the tenant of Banchor Farm barricaded the way to the cemetery and, with the approval of his feudal superior, began to build a farm steading across the road itself. This brought the inevitable storm of protest which was ignored; ultimately the protection of the law was sought. An action was raised in the Edinburgh Court of Session by Peter Cattanach, a lawyer who had local connections. He lodged a plea for suspension and interdict. The demands were quite reasonable. The plaintiffs did not require the destruction of the new buildings, but simply asked for an access road to the cemetery, with permanent rights of way to be made from the highway to the burial ground. A legal battle then ensued with the case being brought before the Lords Ordinary who decided that the folk of Newtonmore had a just case to present. The outcome was that the latter got rather more than their original request for access. Not only were they given the rights of access to Cladh Brighde, but the road was to be constructed at the expense of the respondent. Instead of a footpath, a proper road was to be made to a uniform width of 12 feet and to be maintained with a surface fit for the passage of vehicles.

Finally, to ensure that no future encroachment should be made upon legal rights, a public notice was required to be erected. This notice can still be seen, just to the east of Calder Bridge. It reads: 'An Rathad Daingnichte le lach. Gu Cladh Brighde' (The Roadway Established by Law. To St Bride's Graveyard). The notice is a silent public witness to the manner in which common rights may be established and enforced by law against would-be usurpation. It serves, too, as an interesting memorial to the language which has now all but gone from the day-to-day life and living of Strathspey.

At Pitmain, just before Kingussie, was located the principal inn in Badenoch. It was started by a John MacLean in 1765 and soon became noted for its generous hospitality. Over forty years later, in 1811, it was described as '. . . a very good house, and adjoining it a better garden then I never saw belonging to an inn, if we except some of the public gardens near London. It contained an abundance of fruit, of which we were invited to take part by the landlord, a good-natured man, and very fond of boasting his intimacy with the nobility'. The inn was the annual scene of the great social occasion, a grand dinner and ball, which followed the cattle sale at the Pitmain Tryst. Little of the former inn now remains save its walls, which form part of a steading, and a line of trees marking the boundary of the former garden.

Just south of Pitmain, on the left-hand side of the road going north, is Ballachroan, a group of rather stark buildings. This was the home of Captain John Macpherson, called the 'Black Officer'. He was much disliked in the locality for his role as a recruiting officer, engaged in the business of pressing men for army service. He was also supposed to deal in the Black Arts.

He died, with a hunting companion, on Christmas Day 1799 after a mysterious avalanche swept over his hunting lodge in the remoteness of Gaick. The full story of how the Black Officer got his come-uppance from the Devil is recounted in Affleck Gray's book, *Legends of the Cairngorms*.

CHAPTER 4

Kingussie to Aviemore

In a guidebook of some fifty years ago, the writer said of Kingussie that, due to the pine woods which abound in the vicinity, 'the air of the place is highly beneficial to sufferers of chest complaints'. The village, the capital of Badenoch, stands some 750 feet above sea level and it is not quite one's imagination which senses a feeling of exhilaration. The towering summit of Creag Dubh to the west climbs 2600 feet into the sky and offers an excellent viewpoint of the whole of the Spey Valley and the peaks of the Cairngorms. The name Kingussie is derived from the Gaelic: The Head of the Pinewood.

Kingussie was the ancient Kirktown of the Castle of Ruthven, just across the Spey to the east. A Charter of Barony was granted to the settlement as far back as 1451 but the scattering of houses which then existed did not really come together as an identifiable community until 1799. In that year, on 21 January, an advertisement appeared in the *Aberdeen Journal*: 'The Duke of Gordon being desirous to have a village erected near the church of Kingussie in Badenoch will give every degree of encouragement to tradesmen, manufacturers and shop keepers who may be inclined to settle there'. Then the growth began.

Kingussie, as a recognisable settlement, can actually go back to AD 565, when an ancient chapel, dedicated to St Columba of Iona, was established. About the year 1200 Kingussie was created a parish under the jurisdiction of Muriach, the historical Parson of Kingussie. When his brother died without issue, he became head of his family and succeeded to the Chiefship of Clan Chattan.

He obtained a dispensation from the Pope of the time and married a daughter of the Thane of Cawdor, by whom he had five sons; surnames about this time having become hereditary, Mac-pherson (son of the parson) became the distinguishing clan name, which accounts for the southern end of the Spey

Valley being the home ground of the Macphersons. The churchyard of the old church, Eaglais nan Colum Cille, in Mill Road, just north of the centre of Kingussie, is chock full of Macpherson stones which can still be seen, though no doubt many older slabs have now sunk into the ground. One stone is erected to the memory of Captain Clark whose wife was a daughter of William Shaw of Dalnavert; his grandson became Sir John A. Macdonald, Prime Minister of Canada. Another stone, that of Lt John Macpherson of the 78th Regiment, tells us he was an orderly sergeant to General Wolfe at the Battle of Quebec and fought on the Heights of Abraham. Thus far flung are the natives of Strathspey.

Before the advent of the railway in 1880, Kingussie was the centre of a weaving and spinning industry, supported by the Duke of Gordon, but it failed to sustain itself and went into decline. Then the railway came to transform Kingussie into a tourist centre. Visitors discovered the delights of the Cairngorms. Other visitors came to the area for the shooting, arriving in large parties for the 'glorious twelfth' of August, on which day it was open season for the unfortunate grouse. The rich built themselves villas as holiday homes. Between 1880 and 1900 a sum estimated at £200,000 was spent on erecting these large houses which can be seen today in their Victorian splendour. The owner arrived by train with family and servants, and often with a private wagon loaded with coal. The prosperity brought to Kingussie by this influx lasted until the First World War when the flow of visitors slackened off. The Second World War virtually killed Kingussie as a tourist centre.

However, visitors began to trickle back, and today Kingussie's streets echo former bustling times. A lesson was learned, however, and realising that tourism could not always form a stable economic base, attempts were made to introduce other elements into the economy. An industrial estate was set up which now houses units producing items varying from crafts to precision engineering and bone china goods.

Perhaps the main attraction in Kingussie is 'Am Fasgadh', the Highland Folk Museum. The museum started life in 1935 with the late Dr Isobel F. Grant deciding to organise an institution similar to those she had seen in Scandinavia. There she found a healthy attitude to the preservation of the things of bygone years;

Ruthven Barracks, near Kingussie. Though now deserted, the building is in a fair state of preservation. It is best to visit the Barracks after one has read something of the history. In that way, one can bring the imagination easily into play and perhaps chance a mental game of chess with the Auld One, as did the Wolf of Badenoch. *(Courtesy Scottish Tourist Board)*

in Scotland there was nothing. She had a rather disheartening start in an old church building on the island of Iona, after which she moved her growing collection to Laggan Bridge. Then, in 1944, she moved to the 'Old Lodge' in Kingussie, a white-harled Victorian residence which has been the home of the Museum ever since. From humble beginnings it has been developed and extended and now is the foremost museum of its kind in Scotland.

On display are many items of interest to the naturalist, the sportsman and social historian. That may sound 'academic'. In fact, the museum introduces us to the world of yesteryear, the world of our own forefathers, with the emphasis on the everyday life of ordinary people. A large part of the Museum is given over to demonstrating the harmony with which man in the Highlands lived with natural things.

There are many beautiful examples of home-made wooden vessels made from birch and fir. Brooms and brushes are made from heather twigs, rushes, bent-grass and moss. Ropes are woven from horse hair, rushes and heather fronds as well as the roots of trees and shrubs. The sides of cupboards, cabinets and chairs and constructed from oak scrub. Primitive looms, spinning wheels, wool combs, spindles, cords and implements for scutching flax are on display, as are locally produced textiles and linens. There is a complete set of pearl-fisher's implements including the clap-stick and flat-bottomed flask which tinkers used when searching the bed of the River Spey for its pearls. To add that essential note of authenticity, and to tantalise the taste buds, a working kitchen offers griddle-baked scones and pancakes.

Outside the Museum are displays which demonstrate the great dependence of the old Highland population on the wild life of the countryside for the necessities of life. Farm life is well featured, with working implements and machines. In the grounds there is a replica of a Lewis 'Black House', constructed under the supervision of an old islander who made the journey from Lewis to Kingussie for the purpose. Also to be found in the grounds are a turf house and clack mill driven by water and making the characteristic 'clacking' sound.

Just across the River Spey from Kingussie are the gaunt but imposing ruins of Ruthven Barracks, sitting on a man-made

Balavil House on Speyside. *(Photograph: Hamish Brown)*

mound. The 'Red Place' commands one of the major crossing sites of the Spey and has thus had a rich and chequered history. Now in a ruined state, but still exuding an atmosphere of the past, the barracks are what has been left of the original fortification after the Jacobites blew it up in 1746. The mound, however, has had a structure on it for centuries.

It was originally the base of power of the mighty Comyns, then Lords of Badenoch; later it served as the main stronghold of the Gordons who bought the Lordship of Badenoch from the King in 1452. In the sixteenth century a new structure replaced Ruthven Castle but was itself demolished in 1689. Then in 1718 the Government erected on the site a new building to be used as a staging barracks for troops and horses.

Ruthven has had many visitors in its day, including Mary, Queen of Scots, as well as Cameron of Lochiel and MacDonald of Keppoch, both of whom were imprisoned there in 1546 by the Earl of Huntly. General Wolfe, of Quebec fame, the Marquis of Montrose and Generals Monk and Wade were all familiar with Ruthven in one way or another. The Barracks, built originally to police the unruly Highlanders and the

Jacobite forces after the 'Fifteen' Rising, fell eventually to the supporters of the same cause some thirty years later. Fortunately for us in the present day, they did not completely destroy such a magnificent landmark.

When the Jacobites assembled at Ruthven in 1746, immediately after their defeat at Culloden, they expected to carry on the campaign; instead they received the message to disperse, which they did after blowing up the buildings so that they could not be used to house English redcoats. But this was not the first encounter the garrison had had with the Jacobites. In the previous years the Barracks were successfully held against an attack by the Highlanders. The defending party were troops left behind by Sir John Cope when he marched north to Inverness, instead of making his way to Fort Augustus across the Corrieyairack Pass.

A sergeant and twelve men found themselves confronted by some 300 Highlanders on 30 August 1745. On being asked to surrender, the sergeant replied that he was too old a soldier to surrender a garrison of such strength without a bloody nose. Sergeant Molloy was as good as his word. He managed to repel a number of attacks and lost only one man 'shot through the head by foolishly holding his head too high over the parapet, contrary to orders'. There was no small sigh of relief when the Jacobites decided to leave Ruthven alone.

It was a different story in February 1746 when the Jacobites launched another attack. This time the attack command was taken by Gordon of Glenbucket who, after three days and a brave defence, managed to obtain the surrender of the inmates on honourable terms. They were allowed to march away, a quite different picture from the events which occurred after Culloden two months later, when even the Highland wounded were killed where they lay and those who surrendered voluntarily were despatched without delay.

The Barracks consist of two parallel buildings of equal length running nearly east-west, connected by two buildings of lesser height lying in transverse direction, and all forming a complete square large enough to accommodate two companies of men. There was, besides, a fairly large house which served as a stable for a number of horses.

Today the Barracks stand in splendid isolation and give little

James 'Ossian' Macpherson, a detail from the painting on glass in the Clan Macpherson Museum, Newtonmore. The artist is unknown. *(Photograph: Hamish Brown)*

hint of their turbulent history. Nor do they hint at the event in 1394 which saw the death of the Wolf of Badenoch in the old Ruthven Castle which stood on the mound. Of all the historical characters associated with Strathspey, the Wolf of Badenoch stands out above many; he stalks some of the blackest pages in Scotland's history. He was the natural son of King Robert II and was known as Alasdair Mor mac an Righ, Big Alexander, son of the King. Even in the barbarous days in which he lived he was regarded as a monster and was feared both far and wide. He died in 1394 and is buried at Dunkeld, in Perthshire. In his time he was Lord of Badenoch, Earl of Buchan and his brother's royal deputy in the north of Scotland. When he deserted his wife, the Countess of Ross, she appealed for redress to the Bishop of Moray, who gave judgement in her favour. Alexander, in return, seized some of the Bishop's lands, for which deed he was excommunicated.

In savage fury, the Wolf of Badenoch, bent on revenge, swooped down from his stronghold castle of Lochindorb and sacked and burned the towns of Forres and Elgin, the latter being the ecclesiastical heart of the Bishopric of Moray. He rode with his men into the sleeping town of Elgin one dark night and set off a series of fires, mainly the College and Canon's houses, and the Hospital of the Maison Dieu. The terrified burghers of Elgin fled with their families into the surrounding countryside. Tradition has it that some of these, like Lot's wife, looked back at the sight of the burning Cathedral, with its Gothic windows a tracery of stone against the flames, and were frozen in their tracks with horror. Begun in 1224, the building was one of Scotland's most magnificent structures, and its wanton destruction was unforgivable.

Alexander's father called on his son to do penance for his crime at the door of the Church of the Blackfriars in Perth. This the Wolf of Badenoch did, in the presence of his father, the King, nobles and many church dignitaries; the Wolf was then finally pardoned and received back into the Church. However, Alexander's repentance was only skin deep.

One legend concerns his death in 1394. He was visited in Ruthven Castle by a tall man dressed in black who desired to play a game of chess with him. Hour after hour the game was played until it seemed that time itself was standing still in anticipation of the game's outcome. Suddenly the mysterious visitor moved a piece. 'Check', he said, 'Checkmate' and rose from the game table. His words were accompanied by a clap of thunder, followed by a storm of hail and lightning. The castle was rent by terrible sounds until the morning, when silence reigned.

The 'Drive Round' section of the Highland Wildlife Park, Kincraig. *(Photograph: David Gowans)*

But in that pall of silence, the Wolf of Badenoch's men were found outside the walls dead and blackened as though struck by lightning. Of their leader there was no sign, until his body was found in the banqueting hall. It was unharmed save for one feature: all the nails in his boots had been torn out. Two days later a funeral procession started from the castle; bier after bier was carried out. But no sooner had the last of them been added to the procession than another great storm started; it was concluded that the wrath of the heavens was centred on the coffins. The problem was solved by six strong men taking the Wolf's coffin to the rear: it had originally led the procession. No sooner had this been done than the storm ceased as quickly as it had started. The procession was then able to proceed. Afterwards the local people told of seeing weird lights in the castle at night, with the Wolf of Badenoch replaying his last game of chess with the Devil.

Before a bridge was built across the Spey, the only means of crossing the river from Ruthven to Kingussie was either to ford the river, which was a dangerous exercise, or else cross by the ferryboat, the fare being one penny. The ferryman was a person of some consequence in the community, but rather unprincipled. One Communion Sunday, when the Spey was in spate, a large number of folk gathered to be taken across the river. With an eye to the main chance, the ferryman upped his price from one penny to sixpence.

Despite pleadings from the gathered fold who were desperate to celebrate Communion in Kingussie, he refused to lower his price. Being poor, they could not afford the fare and so turned back home. But the incident did not go unnoticed. When it came to the attention of a church dignitary, he went to the ferryman and scolded him for being so grasping. 'For this greed, vengeance will overtake you here and in the hereafter. You will be deprived of your living, your house and your land, and be sure of this: you will die an unnatural death, and your body will be devoured by beasts.'

This strange prophecy was soon fulfilled. A year later a bridge was built over the Spey and the ferry went out of business. The ferryman worked at odd jobs but never earned enough to keep himself and his family. He finally managed to get work at an old meal mill which stood near the centre of Kingussie High Street. The prophecy was being fulfilled. One day he was sent to close the mill sluice. To do this he had to walk a narrow plank over a pigsty. When he failed to return the miller went to investigate and found, to his horror, that the ferryman had slipped off the plank and landed among the pigs; the terrified animals then attacked the ferryman and killed him.

Just off the road north out of Kingussie is the War Memorial. In 1920, when the site was being excavated to take the foundations of the structure, calcified human remains were found. Local tradition came up with a possible source: the Witch of Laggan who was reputed to have been burned to death some 200 years previously. She had the ability to change her form into a cat, deer and other animals and kept the good folk of Strathspey in an understandable state of fear and alarm.

Just past the village of Lynchat is the estate and Adam mansionhouse of Balavil, a Gaelic adaptation of the French 'Belleville'. This was the home of another James Macpherson

The Aviemore complex now catering for the tourist industry. Though its impact has been both social and economic, this picture shows that it is easy to escape into the surrounding countryside if one's spirit yearns for a brief communing with nature in the woodlands, the hills and the mountains of the Cairngorms. *(Courtesy Scottish Tourist Board)*

whose name is prominent in eighteenth-century European literature.

In the middle of the eighteenth century the attention of the educated classes in Europe was brought sharply to bear on a group of poems translated from Gaelic and said to be of the same age as the works of Homer the Greek. The poems were produced by James Macpherson of Kingussie and they brought about a revolution in European literary tradition, the echoes of which are still as vibrant today as they were in 1762 when *Ossian* was launched on an unsuspecting world.

James Macpherson was born in the now derelict hamlet of Ruthven in 1738 and was educated in the village school there, where he was later to become its headmaster. He received his higher education at Inverness and at the Universities of Aberdeen and Edinburgh, which he turned to excellent use in his future careers. When he was twenty years of age he published a poem called *The Highlander,* which was obscure and based on a mixture of Greek and Gothic mythology. It, somewhat deservedly, was ignored. However, two years later he presented fragments of ancient Gaelic poetry which caused no end of a stir. While genius shone through the verses, they also bore the stamp of a rhythm associated only with heroic poetry. The result was that a public subscription was raised to enable Macpherson to travel throughout the Highlands and Islands of Scotland to collect other fragments of ancient poetry. In 1762 he presented to the world the results of his mission in *Fingal* which he suggested was composed by Ossian, the son of Fingal. The book was a bestseller and its reputation spread like wildfire throughout Britain and Europe.

Fingal contributed to the Romantic Movement in European literature which inspired writers and composers, including Goethe and Wagner, to produce a new kind of literature and music. Napoleon Bonaparte is said to have carried a volume of *Fingal* everywhere on his campaigns, and it was these poems which persuaded him to re-establish the Scots College in Paris, which had been destroyed in the French Revolution. Macpherson was lionised wherever he went.

In 1763 a second volume entitled *Temora* appeared which, instead of enhancing Macpherson's reputation, had the opposite effect: scholars became suspicious of the authenticity of the poems. When asked to produce the original documents from which he professed to translate the ancient Gaelic into English, Macpherson refused. Latter-day research has in fact confirmed that Macpherson had simply made a good job of restoring and restructuring old Gaelic epic poems. He had claimed, somewhat misguidedly, that the poems were translations. In fact, they were productions which gave the general meaning of the Ossianic verses, told in Macpherson's own words and with additions of his own, which he inserted in order to support his belief that the poems had originally formed part of a single epic, comparable to the Odyssey.

Truth is mixed up with fancy here. It has been reasonably suggested that a poet named Ossian did live in the third century AD and that the heroes mentioned in *his* works were real people, although many of their deeds were 'written up' to make a good story. Even today there are tradition-bearers in

This is what it's all about: home-grown ski slopes to entice both the beginner and the experienced skier. Not all winters produce snow in the quantity and quality shown in this picture. During 1988-89, the snow came late in the spring. *(Courtesy Scottish Tourist Board)*

the Highlands and Islands who can recite Ossian's poems – people who have learned the verses orally, the traditional way. The poems were in fact generally known throughout Scotland, although they survived longest in the Gaelic-speaking areas on the western seaboard.

After the appearance of 'Temora', Macpherson's reputation waned. He received rather rough treatment, but managed to overcome this to become a British Governor overseas and then returned to reside in London. He produced a *History of Great*

Britain and an English translation of the Illiad, which the critics inevitable panned. In 1780 he was returned as a Member of Parliament for Camelford, and again in 1784 and 1790. Eventually he retired to his native Badenoch where he bought a small estate on which he built a large house, designed by Adam, standing on the site of the ancient Castle of Rait, near a stone circle, an appropriate juxtaposition of the present with the past, which was a characteristic of his own life.

He died in 1796 and was laid to rest in 'Poets' Corner' in Westminster Abbey. His reputation in Badenoch rests, not on his despoiled literary aspirations, but on his generosity to the poorer tenants of his Balavil estate, and his selfless efforts to have the forfeited Cluny Macpherson lands restored to the family of Ewan Macpherson, attainted for his part in the Forty-five Rising. The present Balavil House was burnt and partially rebuilt in 1903. The family obelisk memorial can be seen across the road from Balavil.

Another Macpherson, who lived at Balavil, is now becoming recognised as a wildlife pioneer photographer. He was Harry Brewster Macpherson who published *The Home Life of the Golden Eagle* in 1909. This is recognised as a pioneer study of the bird's behaviour and is still referred to by specialists. He was unusual in that, at a time when others were busy slaughtering wild life, he was studying it and capturing it for posterity with his camera. A Balavil Society has been set up in Arbroath, where he lived, with the aim of giving Macpherson the recognition he deserves.

Just south of Balavil, on a ridge to the west of the A9 above Lynchat is *An Uamh Mhor* (the big cave), generally known as the Cave of Raitts. It is marked on the OS map as a souterrain. The name Raitts is derived from a Gaelic word which means a place set apart for religious worship. An old Irish word, 'rath', means a place for living inside a hill, which is apt for the Cave.

It is about 70 feet long, 8 feet wide and 7 feet high. It was put to various uses throughout its long history. A number of fugitives from the aftermath of Culloden found safety and shelter there. Later it was occupied by a gang of robbers in 1773, a team of ruffians which was broken up after their leader was hanged in Inverness.

Rothiemurchus Forest looking into the Spey Valley from the road to Tullochgrue. *(Photograph: Hamish Brown)*

The main story attached to the cave concerns the MacNivens, a clan who were vassals of the Earls of Badenoch, who held the lands in the vicinity. When King Robert the Bruce cleared out the Comyn Earls he gave the lands to the Macphersons, who had been loyal to him in his campaigns to gain the Crown of Scotland. The MacNivens naturally resented this and made a point of harassing the Macphersons at every opportunity. Rather than initiate a long feud, the latter sent a daughter of the chief to parley with the MacNivens with a view to reaching an amicable solution to the problem. She was sent, rather than a man who would have been killed outright. But instead of being accorded the dignity due to her sex and rank, the poor girl was badly treated and sent home in humiliation.

This insult was too much for the Macphersons who decided to settle the matter once and for all time. One version of the story relates how most of the MacNivens were killed, but a handful escaped. This small band haunted the area but could never be found. In the following months one of the Macphersons became suspicious of a hut that had been erected at Raitts. To investigate matters he disguised himself as a beggar to gain entry to the hut. Inside were two women who gave him some bread and then told him to be off. But he pretended to be ill and put on such a convincing performance that the women alowed him to stay for the night. While he slept with half an eye open, he noticed the women busy baking large quantities of scones which they placed in a cupboard. Yet the cupboard always seemed to be empty: the scones were feeding more than two mouths. The next day he left and reported back to the Macphersons who mounted a raiding party and arrived at the hut duly armed. The hut was pulled down and the remaining MacNivens were discovered, to be massacred to a man.

At Kincraig is the Highland Wildlife Park, opened in 1972. The aim of the Park is to display, in natural surroundings, the wildlife of Scotland, both past and present. The Park extends to over 200 acres, including a small section of one of the roads built by General Wade. It can be seen as a grassed track running towards the Park's exit gate. It then crosses the approach road to the Park, continues for a quarter of a mile and disappears into the Meadowburn Quarry.

The animals on show include red deer, bison, Soay sheep (from the remote island of St Kilda), Highland cattle, Alpine ibex and roe deer. Other species, like the wolf and brown bear, were once common in Scotland. Since the Park was opened, it has become something of a focal point for migrating and breeding birds. Parts of the Park allow cars to travel slowly through, provided that passengers remain inside. The Park is operated by the Royal Zoological Society of Scotland and, as such, along with Edinburgh Zoo, forms the Scottish National Zoological Collection.

Kincraig itself was originally called Boat of Insh, where one could obtain a ferry to cross the Spey at the north end of Loch Insh. The building of a bridge made the ferry redundant. At one time Loch Insh was known for its pike and salmon. There is a mention of sixty salmon being taken in at one haul: halcyon days compared to the present when salmon are so scarce due to factory fishing and netting in the free-for-all oceanic waters outside territorial limits.

The Loch Insh marshes are now a nature reserve. The acres of overspill waters provide an ideal environment for wild

Glenmore Lodge, the National Outdoor Training Centre under the Cairngorms. *(Photograph: Hamish Brown)*

swans, whose dramatic calls herald the arrival of winter on Speyside. The marshes are an important wintering place for wild Whooper swans. The 1200-acre reserve, half of which is owned by the Royal Society for the Protection of Birds and half leased from local owners, provides a sanctuary for nearly ten per cent of all the Whooper swans which come to Britain in the winter. The largest of our migratory fowl, they breed in Iceland and arrive in Speyside in early October, having made the long haul over the dangerous waters of the North Atlantic.

Tor Alvie, on the east side of the A9, is a wooded hill on the summit of which is the Waterloo Monument, erected by the Marquis of Huntly in 1815 to the memory of the soldiers of the 42nd or Royal Regiment and the 92nd or Gordon Highlanders who fell at the Battle of Waterloo in June 1815. The Tor also supports the monument to George V, and the last Duke of Gordon who died in 1836. In his time he was a general in the Army and Governor of Edinburgh Castle.

The obelisk has inscriptions in Gaelic, English and Latin.

Another monument, this time in the grounds of Kinrara House on the banks of the Spey, commemorates Jane, Duchess of Gordon, who died in 1812. The monument lists the 'favourable' marriages through which her five daughters strengthened the aristocracy.

Situated on a promontory of Loch Alvie is one of the most attractive churches in the Highlands. It is dedicated to St Drostan and the site is reckoned to be one of the first of the early Celtic religious foundations in Speyside. There is a date of 1380 for the chapel built on the site of an earlier religious cell. It has in its time undergone many changes. It once had a gallery and a box pew where the Duke and Duchess of Gordon sat, on a higher level than their tenants. In 1880 the building was improved considerably. During the renovation work the remains of 150 bodies were discovered. Who they were and in what circumstances they died is unknown, though the prevalent theory is that they were victims of some battle. Yet there is no local tradition of such a conflict. The skeletons, all found lying head to head, were subsequently reinterred in the churchyard and marked with a granite stone bearing the inscription: 'Buried here are the Remains of 150 Human Bodies Found, October 1880, beneath the Floor of this Church. Who they were, When they lived, How they Died, Tradition Notes not. Their Bones are Dust, Their good Swords Rust, their souls are with the Saints we Trust'.

Just before the road enters Aviemore, the little village of Lynwilg conveys a peaceful atmosphere. But it was a different story in 1789. The source of the trouble in that year was a Colonel Thornton, an eccentric sportsman from Yorkshire who shot every single species of wildlife that settled in his gun sights.

He rented some land at Raitts, from which base he made many shooting excursions into the immediate area. When that novelty dulled, he wrote to the Duke of Gordon's factor for more land. The factor wrote: 'As Colonel Thornton now insists on having full possession, I have been obliged to bring a removal order against the subtenants at Linwailg [now Lynwilg] in order to make room for him . . . I would try settling with the subtenants for the remainder of the farm and reserve a few acres for the Colonel at the east end of Loch Alvie, which was

Sailing lessons on Loch Morlich. *(Photograph: Hamish Brown)*

the spot he seemed fondest of'. Thus the Colonel became one of the first contributors to Highland depopulation.

About 150 years ago the inn at Aviemore was described thus: 'there was no such inn upon the road, fully furnished, neatly kept, excellent cooking, the most attentive of landlords, all combined to raise the fame of Aviemore. Travellers pushed on from the one side, stopped short at the other, to sleep in this comfortable inn'. Then came the opening of the Highland Railway between Perth and Forres, and the inn fell into disuse and was closed. However, the geographical position of Aviemore was to be an asset in its favour and the later opening of the direct line to Inverness via Carrbridge made Aviemore an important railway junction which was recognised in the new houses that were soon built to accommodate visitors. Its situation was always extolled: 'As one steps from the train at Aviemore after a long night journey from the South, one's travel-tiredness is instantly dispelled by the wonderful air of Upper Speyside. It blows across to the Strath direct from the high Cairngorms that stand mist-swept or clear, according to the weather, a few miles to the south. Spring and summer often come together in this Highland glen. One week the birches are leafless as at mid-winter, then comes a succession of warm sunny days when the hill burns of the Cairngorms are full to the brim with snow water and the air is balmy even to the hill tops. The birches instantly respond to the summer spell, and the trees clothe themselves with filmy green and drench the air with their perfume. After a shower at the end of an early June day the scent of the Aviemore birches is one of the most exquisite things in nature'.

Despite the massive development of tourist facilities in the area, the landscape is still able to provide that same kind of atmosphere and, despite the scarring which has occurred in some places, there is still the chance for those seeking solace to find it without going too far off the beaten track. The landscape in fact still dominates the visits of over one million people a year to the area around Aviemore.

The hill of Craigellachie immediately to the west of Aviemore marks the dividing point between Badenoch and Strathspey. The birchwood above the Aviemore Centre is now a National Nature Reserve which offers a nature trail, taking the visitor on foot up through the wood from which there are commanding views across the Spey to the Cairngorms.

Until the 1960s Aviemore was a small village with a couple of hotels, including the Aviemore Station Hotel which was burnt to the ground a few years before. That fire may have been significant because it ended one era and started an astonishing period of development the nature of which the Highlands had never before experienced.

It began in a small way with an investigation into the possibilities of winter sports on the Cairngorms. A group of hoteliers got together to plan for an extension for the short summer season. Along with the Cairngorm Sports Development Ltd. (which built the White Lady chairlift in 1963 and the newer Coire na Ciste chairlift), the local initiative transformed the winter scene in the Spey Valley. Before long hotels were finding they could afford to stay open all year round. This change did not go unnoticed by the Scottish Development Department, in Edinburgh's St Andrew's House, to say nothing of big commercial interests.

The latter in particular had noticed how much had been achieved with local initiative and with little outside financial assistance. The question was raised: what could be achieved with a massive injection of capital? While the answer to that question was being mulled over, another question was raised:

what harm might be done to the area if mushroom development was allowed? In time the commercial interest and the conservationists were to take sides about development, particularly in the Cairngorms. One of the main initiators of speculative interests in the Spey Valley was the late Lord Fraser of Allander, who was known for his habit of referring to natural scenery and wildlife as 'the merchandise'. This displayed an attitude of mind which tended to confirm fears that profit would be pushed far ahead of other considerations. But powerful interests were involved. Political circles saw that a holiday complex based in Aviemore would satisfy three commercial and altruistic aims: to create a tourist magnet; to boost Scotland's tourist industry by building a centre that would attract overseas as well as home visitors; and to encourage economic development of this part of the Highlands by creating jobs and commercial opportunities that would stop the steady drift of population to the south.

Thus politics and commerce combined to create the first holiday complex at a cost of £2.5 million, though the final cost was to soar to nearer £5 million. There was, however, more than a hint of unholy haste. Insufficient research had been carried out at the planning stage to find out just how big a development the Spey Valley could absorb. Planners were accused by conservationists of putting the cart before the horse by attracting tourists into the area, solving long-term problems with short-term solutions. In brief, planners had introduced an element of urban planning, the only expertise they had, instead of planning for the countryside as a whole.

Meanwhile the project went ahead, to be built on a seventy-five-acre site below the line of the Monadhliah mountains: a complex of hotels, roads, chalet accommodation, a caravan site, a theatre-cum-cinema, ice-rink, shops, restaurant and other facilities. In addition a self-contained new community was built in the middle of the existing and older-established Aviemore village.

It took many years before the investors were able to see a reasonable return on their capital outlay. On the other side of the coin, the resident population increased significantly, accompanied by an equally significant increase in the spending power of the tourist influx. While the development was centred on Aviemore, the rest of the Spey Valley looked as though it might be neglected; but this problem was solved when the Highlands and Islands Development Board began to invest in a scheme which diffused the tourist industry throughout the area, from Dalwhinnie and Laggan northwards to Grantown on Spey. This was an important move. The Badenoch district, which had been losing its population up until 1961, started to enjoy a population boost: 3000 in the decade to 1976.

Today the visitor to the Spey Valley has access to an extremely wide variety of activities from the strenuous to the passive, and most of a high quality. Accommodation and visitor facilities are continually monitored to ensure that the area's reputation for value for money is maintained. All tastes are catered for from discos and après-ski, to simply trekking on foot around the evidence of the area's prehistoric past in the form of cairns and standing stones. And what is important is that the scent of Aviemore birches, so eloquently described and appreciated last century, still delights the nostrils.

To the east of Aviemore lies Rothiemurchus (the Great Plain of the Firs) which has, for 400 years, been in the unbroken possession of the Grants of Rothiemurchus. The estate has been developed in recent years to become 'visitor-orientated'. But this has not resulted in brash commercialisation of the estate's natural attractions; rather the developments have been designed to harmonise with the surroundings. Rothiemurchus Forest contains one of the few remaining areas of naturally regenerating Caledonian Pine Forest in the British Isles.

Though most of the Forest is dominated by the native Scots pine, other species, such as larch, fir, spruce and birch, are to be found. Conservation methods are applied with both tact and sensitivity, so that little offends the eye. Yet the land is managed, rather than thrashed, to produce maximum return. Management practices within the Forest vary according to potential timber yields, extraction costs, nature conservation interests, vegetation type and the existing stock of trees; care is also taken with scenic amenity.

Access to the estate is gained just south of Aviemore, passing through Inverdruie. At one time this little village was the centre of a large timber operation. Massive quantities of logs were sawn into deals or planks. The trees were floated down the River Druie from the forest of Rothiemurchus. Many logs were floated onto the River Spey in great rafts to arrive at the mouth of the Spey to feed the shipyard at Kingston. One main attraction at Inverdruie is the trout fish farm: an 8-acre artificial loch with some 250,000 trout. A well-stocked fishing loch offers amateur anglers a chance to try their hand.

Contained within the Rothiemurchus estate is Loch an Eilean which saw, in 1899, the last of that magnificent bird, the osprey, after it had been shot and its eggs collected. That was the last of the bird until its return, much later, mainly to Loch Garten. The castle on a small island in the loch was once a stronghold of the Comyns, a clan who held no little sway over Strathspey until they were ousted. Until 200 years ago, the castle could be reached by a causeway which disappeared when the loch was dammed to allow sufficient water to build up before a sluice gate was opened for the floating of logs down to the Spey. A nearby wood-boring mill once produced lengths of Scots pine for use as water pipes. In the eighteenth century many of these pipes were used for London's water supply.

Between Inverdruie and Loch an Eilean is a small place called Croft where the young Laird of Grant lived along with a housekeeper who bore him three children. This affair was not much to the liking of the Laird's father who called in a local character, Black Sandy Grant, to get his advice on how to deal with the problem. Telling the old Laird to leave things in his hands, Black Sandy got himself up in a disguise and waylaid the unfortunate housekeeper and cut off one of her ears. Of course, she was unable to identify her attacker and Sandy, having received the thanks of the Laird of Grant, moved himself to Grantown for safe-keeping. But not long afterwards he was involved in a fight with a cattle drover which ended in the drover being left for dead near Spey Bridge.

This time, Sandy found himself a marked man. To escape the vengeance of the drover's friends, he emigrated to America There his obvious talents for enterprise found a place and he became moderately prosperous. Fame was to come to Clan Grant in the form of his son, Ulysses S. Grant, born in Ohio in 1822, who became President of the United States. President Grant visited his father's homeland before he died in 1855, and no doubt reflected on the quirks of fate which had brought him to that high position.

There is also a Canadian association with this area: Helen Shaw, from Dalnavert just up the river, emigrated to Canada and gave birth to a son who was to become Sir John Macdonald, the first Prime Minister of Canada.

The prominent stone pillar at the T-junction of the road leading to Loch an Eilean is the Martineau Monument. It was erected to the memory of Dr James Martineau who was one of the leaders of the Unitarian Movement which, contradicting the doctrine of the Trinity, maintained that God is one person. He and his family lived for a long time in Rothiemurchus and established a school of drawing and carving. When he died in 1900, the pupils of the school worked the carvings on the memorial. It is similar in design to the Eleanor Crosses which were set up in England to mark the route of the funeral procession of Eleanor, wife of Edward I of England.

On the eastern marches of the Rothiemurchus estate is The Queen's Forest, or Glen More Forest Park. The former name came into being in 1935 to commemorate the Silver Jubilee of King George V and Queen Mary. The land had been purchased some twelve years previously by the Forestry Commission and the planting of the woodlands has been a continuous process since that date. Now some 4000 acres grow trees ranging from one to forty years, along with the remnants of the old Caledonian Scots pine, which can be seen in groups or single trees of great age, up to 200 years.

Glenmore itself was formerly a royal forest and latterly the hunting ground of the Stewarts of Kincardine. It is now the home of the National Outdoor Training Centre which is sponsored by the Scottish Sports Council and provides courses intended to introduce, or further develop, skills in adults on a direct tuition basis in a number of outdoor pursuits which vary according to the season. The main feature in the Forest Park is Loch Morlich whose waters offer a wide range of water sports. To the north of Loch Morlich is Reindeer House, the administration base for a herd of reindeer.

The reindeer were once one of the native animals in Scotland, along with the wolf and the bear. The species is supposed to have survived in Caithness until the twelfth century. A reindeer appears on a carved stone of the early

Reindeer are one of the many indigenous animals displayed at the Highland Wildlife Park, Kincraig. *(Photograph: Hamish Brown)*

Christian period found at Grantown on Spey, indicating that the animal was at one time no stranger to the Spey Valley and the Cairngorms.

During the years of last century various attempts were made to reintroduce the reindeer to Scotland, but none was successful. However, the British Reindeer Company thought another try might yield results, and in 1952 some mountain and forest reindeer were placed in the Glenmore Forest. To look after the animals a Lapp from Northern Sweden, the late Mikel Utsi, was placed in charge. Once the reindeer had become acclimatised to their new home, they were herded into an area south of Loch Morlich, enclosing old pine forest and windswept moorland. They seemed to thrive and also proved the point of the whole experiment: could reindeer be established on a commercial basis without the addition to the staple diet of reindeer moss? It seemed that they could, and now, in summer, visitors can see a herd of about one hundred animals, all Scottish-born, roaming over the Ben Macdhui plateau and at Carn Lochain.

Those interested in rummaging around old cemeteries should visit the old parish church of Rothiemurchus and its walled burial ground. It is located at Doune on the road between Inverdruie and Loch an Eilean. Perhaps the most interesting grave is that of Shaw Mor, or Seath Mor Sgorfhiaclach, who was the victor in the battle which took place at the North Inch, Perth, in 1396. The grave is marked by five small stones, said to have been brought from the prehistoric mound at Doune. With them came a prophecy that anyone who removed even one of the stones would die. One man did so and on his way home the River Spey went into a sudden spate and he was drowned while trying to cross the water. He was Robert Scroggie, a footman of the Duke of Bedford, who had taken it upon himself to convince the locals that their superstitious fears were groundless. His gravestone is to be seen in the same churchyard.

The first service to be held in Doune parish church for more than forty years took place in 1977. Before that, some months of hard work went into the restoration of the building as part of a Job Creation Scheme. It is the intention to have a special service every summer to keep the building alive as a church. Some of the old furnishings, including the lectern and the eighteenth-century pewter communion plate, have now found a new lease of life for the first time since 1931.

CHAPTER 5

Aviemore to Grantown

One can travel north out of Aviemore, with its attractions and excitements, in two ways, each offering a chance to go back in time. For those who wish to sense the sight, sounds and pungent smells of a steam train, then it is a simple enough matter to catch one of the trains run by the Strathspey Railway Company. Its station terminus is located behind the main line of Aviemore Station. The five-mile rail journey takes one to Boat of Garten station. The route, though short, runs through countryside which has changed little since the original railway line was built in August 1863.

The road out of Aviemore goes past memorials of an ancient past; they confirm the long period of human habitation which Strathspey has witnessed. Just outside Aviemore there are the ruins of a burial cairn, erected around 1500BC. In the form of a stone circle, the structure was complete until it was robbed for building material in the 1840s. More fortunate is the virtually intact stone circle on the east side of the main railway line, two miles north of Aviemore.

The ancient fort (AD 100) at Avielochan is a strong stone-walled building occupying a rocky promontory on the west side of Strathspey above Loch Vaa. The approach to the fort from the foot of Beinn Ghuilbin takes the form of a narrow neck which is traversed by a high fence erected in recent times to restrict the movement of deer. Just beyond this is the first of a series of ruined walls formed from massive boulders. The next line of defence is a wall, mostly represented by a form of terracing, which girdles the promontory at a level of some 20 feet below the summit. The last line to be encountered is another ruinous wall which encloses the juniper-choked summit which measures about 220 feet long by 80 feet wide.

This fort, along with another one east of Loch Pityoulish, is a prime indication that, at a time before recorded history, the Spey Valley was of particular economic and military importance, probably with a fairly large population which

71

required protection from incursions and raids by land-hungry neighbours.

Jumping some centuries forward in time, there is yet another indication that this area had some importance. This is the oldest road in Strathspey of which there is any record: the *Via Regia*, the King's Road. It is sometimes called Alexander's Road because it is said to have been constructed on the orders of a Scottish king, most likely Alexander II. The date of the building of the road is given as 1263, the year of the Battle of Largs which finally severed Scotland from her painful domination by the Norsemen. Alexander II was involved in repelling Norse raids by the Jarls of Orkney, and it was highly desirable for the movement of defensive troops to prevent the Norsemen from moving south. The road came from the south, over the Drumochter Pass, and kept to the right bank of the Spey, past Rothiemurchus and Pityoulish to the neighbourhood of Achgourish. There it branched off to Tulloch, south of Staor-na-Mannach, which is still called in Gaelic 'Rathad an Righ', the King's Road. The road was by law endowed with a right of way and pasturage so that it could be used for peaceful as well as military traffic.

Although not strictly a village of the River Spey, Carrbridge does rest on the banks of the brawling River Dulnain, whose waters flow from the Monadhliath Mountains to make no small contribution to the flood of the Spey. The village began as a tiny settlement which attached itself to the Bridge of Carr. This was built in 1717 on the orders of General Alexander Grant of Grant, in response to a petition from the local people for a safe means to cross the River Dulnain with burial parties bound for the old churchyard at Duthil. Matters were brought to a head after two local men lost their lives when trying to cross the Dulnain in flood.

The bridge was built for £100, with the specification that it should be of 'ane reasonable Breadth and Height as will Receive the water when in the greatest speat'. It took only six months to build and, though now largely ruinous, its high arch more than impresses both eye and mind. The bridge is a Grade I listed building; for its age it is in´ reasonable structural condition though recent concern has been expressed when it was noticed that one of the keystones from the arch had been knocked out of place.

Boat of Garten station, August 1986. *(Photograph: Robert R F Kinghorn, from* Speyside Railways *by Rosemary A Burgess and Robet R F Kinghorn)*

Carrbridge today is solidly based on catering for the tourist. In the 1950s Karl Fuchs' Austrian Ski School became one of the main catalysts in the development of skiing in the Spey Valley. Then, in 1970, came the Landmark Visitor Centre, set in some thirty acres of native pine forest. It was destroyed by fire in 1973, but an imaginative rescue operation produced what you see today: forest trails, picnic areas, a multi-vision show and exhibition, an adventure playground and Scotland's largest outdoor display of contemporary sculpture. In 1988, a forest tower, 70 feet high, was opened. It forms part of a Scottish Forestry Heritage Park now being developed. The purpose of the Park is to tell the story of the forestry industry in the Scottish Highlands since the eighteenth century.

To the east of Carrbridge is the village of Duthil, with its whitewashed church and the Grant Mausoleum. This was the traditional burial place of the Chiefs of Clan Grant. The old name for this place was 'Gleann a Chearnaich', the Glen of Heroes, from the large number of fighting warriors it produced. Tradition has it that before going off to fight, each man placed a stone on a cairn at Duthil and, if he survived, he returned to remove his own stone. Thus every stone that remained represented a man fallen in battle.

The present church, now unused, dates from 1826. The mausoleum in the churchyard contains the remains of all the Grant Chiefs from 1585 until 1913, when it was closed permanently. It is an imposing structure with its arched doors and ornamental corners, a fitting memorial to a powerful Strathspey clan.

The name Boat of Garten has long lost the visible source of its name: the chain-operated ferry across the River Spey which was replaced by a bridge in 1899. It does, however, retain something of its rural setting as a settlement dating from the opening of the railway in 1863. This brought in floods of tourists whose need for accommodation led to the building of Edwardian period villas and the rebuilding of the old inn to form the present Boat Hotel.

Although the old railway line heading for Forres has now been closed, the station has had new life breathed into it. It is now the terminus of the Aviemore/Boat of Garten Strathspey Railway. The idea of re-opening the Aviemore/Boat of Garten link came from the Highlands and Islands Development Board, in an attempt to diversify the tourist facilities in the Spey Valley. In 1967 the Scottish Railway Preservation Society was asked to put up a scheme and make an offer for the 5-mile stretch of line. But the scheme fell through, to be rescued four years later by a group of railway enthusiasts who formed the Strathspey Railway Company.

This time, backed by grants, loans and private finance, the line was bought. The next step was a programme of restoration, begun in 1972, which included the refurbishment of Boat of Garten station. In addition, a Light Railway Order had to be granted by the Department of the Environment before passengers could be carried in the rolling stock. Much hard work, carried out mainly by volunteers, has gone into making the railway line reflect some of its former glory. There is now an impressive working collection of rolling stock and locomotives. The old Boat station is fully restored with the waiting room converted into a small museum. But above all is the opportunity of taking a journey into the bygone days of steam trains with all the nostalgia which that brings, at least to

One of the superb engines of the Strathspey Railway.
(*Photograph: Hamish Brown*)

an older generation. For the young, it is a door opening into
history.

To the east of Boat of Garten is Abernethy Forest which is a
National Nature Reserve and includes the recently acquired
Dell Wood. The latter forms an important part of the Forest,
and is the largest surviving remnant of the native Caledonian
pinewood which once covered much of the Highlands. The
Dell Wood has a varied appearance: from tall mature pine
stands to scattered trees and open areas where the forest has
been clear-felled. Lochans and burns add to the diversity of the
habitat, which supports a special range of wildlife. Birds of the
native pinewood include capercaillie, crested tit, and Scottish
crossbill, a species found nowhere else in the world.

The highlight of Abernethy Forest must be Loch Garten,
now the home of the osprey, the fish-eating eagle. This bird
has rightly been chosen as a symbol of the Spey Valley, for its
come-back in recent years almost underlines the increased
awareness of the very species which reduced its number in the
Highlands to the point of extinction many years ago. This

come-back was no easy matter, for time and time again the birds were frustrated in their nesting by vandals, and, worse, egg-collectors.

The osprey was once common in the Highlands and attracted the attention of many people with double standards. One such was Charles St John. In one of his books he writes: 'I walked on to look at the osprey's nest in the old castle, and an interesting sight it is, though I lamented the absence of the birds. Why the poor osprey should be persecuted I know not, as it is quite harmless, living wholly on fish, of which everyone knows there is too great an abundance in this country for the most rigid preserver to grudge this picturesque bird his share'. After this great show of concern, St John describes, a few pages later, the shooting of a hen osprey and the taking of two eggs from the nest. Writing of the calling of the distraught male bird he says: 'I was really sorry I had shot her', and further tells us of the fate of the male: 'I am sorry to say that I shot him deliberately in cold blood as he sat'.

St John is actually on record as shooting the last osprey in Sutherland. Not content with this record, he and a friend were busy for several years in succession harrying the osprey eyrie in Loch an Eilean near Aviemore, robbing the nest of eggs. Despite St John's efforts, the osprey returned to Loch an Eilean a number of times, but it was always an attraction for egg-collectors. The year 1899 saw the last attempt of the bird to nest and breed successfully. After that the osprey was extinct so far as the Highlands were concerned.

Then, in 1936 Desmond Nethersole-Thompson, a first-class naturalist of Highland fame, saw single ospreys flying over lochs in Strathspey, but found no evidence of breeding. Thereafter the bird was seen at regular intervals until 1954, when a nest was found and its location kept a tight secret. In the following year a pair was sighted building a nest close to Loch Garten. The come-back had started.

Every spring for over 25 years now ospreys have returned from their winter quarters in Africa to nest at Loch Garten. It has not been a wholly welcome return, for twice the nests have been robbed of eggs. But the protective efforts of the Royal Society for the Protection of Birds have been instrumental in creating an environment which assures the future. Indeed the

Ancient and modern: the two bridges at Carrbridge. Stepping rather cautiously over the River Dulnain, the old bridge has managed to survive the two centuries since it was built in 1776 to allow funeral parties to cross the Dulnain and arrive at the old churchyard at Duthil in comparative safety. *(Courtesy Scottish Tourist Board).*

story of the Speyside ospreys has been recounted worldwide as an example of imaginative nature conservation and interpretation.

The birds at Loch Garten feed almost exclusively on fish, mostly trout and pike. Each bird plunges into the water to catch prey with its talons, which are specially designed to grip the wriggling fish. Throughout the breeding season the male supplies the food. With a wing span of up to five feet, the flying osprey is one of the magnificent wonders of Speyside, rivalled only by the golden eagle.

North of Abernethy Forest is Nethy Bridge, which takes its name from the hump-backed bridge across the River Nethy, one of the Spey's tributaries. The village was not always the quiet settlement it is now. In the early eighteenth century this area was the scene of great activity, when the York Buildings Company of London obtained a lease of the woods of

Abernethy. A furnace was erected, to produce charcoal made from pine trees and to reduce iron ore brought from the Lecht on long strings of pack ponies. Lumber was also floated from Nethy Bridge down to the mouth of the Spey. One local minister of the time was not happy with the Company's employees: 'Their extravagances of every kind ruined themselves and corrupted others. They used to display their vanity by bonfires, tar barrels and opening hogsheads of brandy to the country people, by which five of them died in one night'.

At the turn of this century, nearly 200 years after the Company had collapsed (1735), the 'Iron Mill Croft' still displayed the solid remains of the beams and framework of the original structure, though much had fallen into the river bed by that time. The site can still be seen, however.

Just outside Nethy Bridge is the substantial ruin of Castle Roy. One of the earliest buildings of its kind in Scotland, it has walls seven feet thick which have stood the test of seven centuries. A local tradition has it that a plague-infested treasure lies in the castle environs.

Dulnain Bridge and Skye of Curr form a joint crofting community with Ballintomb, to the east of Dulnain Bridge. If it might be thought that heather comes in only one colour, purple, then the Heather Garden Centre at Skye of Curr will be a welcome surprise. Over the years the Centre has been developed into a landscaped area where over 200 varieties of heather are shown off to great advantage.

In the old days Ballintomb was the assembly ground for rallies of members of Clan Grant. In 1710, when Sir Ludovick Grant passed the clan leadership on to his son, a great gathering of Grants took place, commons and gentlemen 'all armed, wearing whiskers and wearing plaids and tartans of red and green'. It was also, however, a place where the laird's power of 'pit and gallows' was exercised. There is on record, dated September 1697, the trial of three men for stealing cattle and sheep. They were sentenced to be 'brought to the Gallowhill of Ballintomb, and all three hanged upon the gallows of Ballintomb betwict two and four in the afternoon till they be dead'. Another man was sentenced to be 'bound to the gallows at the time of their execution and to have his left ear

Duthil Church and the Grant Mausoleum. *(Photograph: Hamish Brown)*

cut off and to be scourged and banished'. These were tough times!

Just north of an almost semi-circular bend in the River Spey is Grantown on Spey, which owes its origins to the efforts of the Laird of Grant to establish a new economic focal point for the area. The first public notice of the Laird's intention appeared in the *Aberdeen Journal* on Monday 15 April 1765: 'Sir Ludovic Grant and Mr. Grant of Grant propose a TOWN should be erected and will give feus of long leases, and all proper Encouragement to Manufacturers, Tradesmen, or others, sufficiently recommended and attested as to Character and Ability, who incline to settle there ... will find that is a good pleasant country, and well accommodated with all materials for building, lies near plenty of Moss and other Firing, has the Woods of Abernethie and Glenchernick near it, and a fine Limestone Quarry easily wrought. It is particularly well situated for all Manufacturers of Wool or Linen, being a great sheep Country; the Linen Manufactory already introduced, the soil good, and having fine Water and every conveniency for Bleachfields. The situation is also well adapted for Wood Merchants, Carpenters, Cart Wrights, etc, the Wood lying near, and to be had at low Prices, and a very moderate Charge floated down Spey to Garmouth, where Shipping may be easily had . . .'

The new town was to be built on the site of an older settlement. Old Grantown, known as Castletown of Freuchie, was in existence before 1553 and stood about a half-mile south-west of Castle Grant, the ancient sea of the chiefs of Clan Grant.

In 1694 King William III and Queen Mary ordained 'the town formerly called Castletown of Frequhie, now and in all time to come to be called the Town and Burgh of Grant, and to be the principal burgh of regality, a market cross to be erected therein, and proclamations to be made thereat'.

However, this settlement never got off the ground and failed to be revived again in the 1760s. The new venture succeeded, perhaps because of a different set of circumstances. In 1766 the new town was laid out on a grid system of streets ' . . . planned out and marked off ground in lots or tenements for a village upon a barren heath moor, about an English mile or a little more south-west from the house of Castle Grant, and said year some of these lots or tenements were taken and houses erected'. By the 1780s, under the watchful eye of the 'good Sir James', Grantown had become a prosperous centre of the Highland linen industry and had, in addition, become the main market town for a large part of the Spey Valley.

As well as linen, woollen cloths were produced, some of which gained an export market as far afield as West Africa. Towards the end of the century the linen industry here failed, as it did elsewhere, in the face of the competition from cheap cotton from the Americas. But sufficient impetus for growth had been established and the town went on to become one of the finest planned towns in the north of Scotland. Indeed, by the middle of last century it had grown to such an extent that it rivalled Inverness, to become the second largest town in the country. Further impetus was given to Grantown by the visit of Queen Victoria in 1860 (she paid 'an amusing and never to be forgotten visit'). In 1863 the arrival of the railway set the seal on Grantown's reputation as a base for visitors.

As with all the schemes of men, the original inducements

The Heather Heritage Centre, Skye of Curr.
(Photograph: Hamish Brown)

held forth by the promoters were more of a promise than a guarantee. Indeed, had a similar advertisement appeared in the pages of our modern newspapers, the promoters might well have found themselves in court for gilding the lily; for example, 'shipping' was not 'easily had' at Garmouth and the 'materials for building' were not up to the necessary standards. Even so, the present population of some 1600 inhabitants will agree that the town has gained more than it has lost in the two centuries of its existence.

Grantown is a planning delight, particularly the Square, which is a town centre almost without equal in the Highlands. The trees are nearly a century old and carry their age with graceful dignity. The Square, the former market place, was given to the townspeople to mark the bicentenary of the founding of Grantown. Some of the oldest buildings in the town line the Square. At the north-west corner is an eighteenth-century house with double windows, a reminder of the days when houseowners had to pay a window tax. The granite Speyside House, built to replace a former eighteenth-century orphanage, has clean sharp lines which more than please the eye. The clock under the cupola was paid for out of funds collected for soldiers in the Napoleonic Wars; but by the time the fund had reached its target the wars had ended, and the clock was installed as an aide-mémoire for the townspeople.

Just north of Grantown is Castle Grant, originally known as Ballachastell or Castle of Freuchie. For some six centuries it was the home of the chiefs of Clan Grant, ever since Sir John Grant received, in the thirteenth century, a gift from the King of Scots, of part of the lands of Strathspey formerly held by the Comyns. The towers of the castle are the oldest parts of the building, and date from *circa* 1200. One of the towers is reputed to be haunted by the ghost of Lady Barbara, or Barbie, who was walled up alive here for her misdeeds.

Castle Grant was greatly altered in the eighteenth century when John Adam redesigned the north front. When Queen Victoria visited the castle she described it in her *Journal* as 'a very plain-looking house, like a factory'. Other visitors included John Taylor, the 'Penniless Poet', who stayed there in 1618. He anticipated modern sensation-mongering by making a tour of the British Isles with empty pockets and wrote up his observations for the gossip-reading fraternity of his time.

Robert Burns was once a guest in the castle, where he met the 'Bonnie Lesley', whom he later immortalised in song. During the Forty-five Rising, the castle fell into the hands of the Jacobites who occupied it for some days. They did no damage but discovered the well-stocked cellar, the contents of which kept thoughts of fighting out of their minds for a time.

The castle lay empty for a number of years, but is open now to the public from April to September. The estate lands have been renovated and include an adventure playground.

A short mile or so south of Grantown the Old Spey Bridge spans the River Spey. Built in 1754, it carries the old military road from Blairgowrie to Fort George near Inverness. At the time of its construction it was the only permanent crossing place over the Spey between Garvamore and the sea.

CHAPTER 6

Cromdale to Kingston

As I cam in by Auchindoun,
A little wee bit frae the town,
When tae the Highlands I was boun',
To view the Haughs o Cromdale,

I met a man in tartan trews,
I spier'd at him what was the news;
Quoth he, 'The Highland army rues
That ere they came to Cromdale'.

So runs the folk song which is as popular today as it was
nearly three centuries ago, so crushing was the defeat of the
Highlanders who had risen in support of King James VII and
II and who had annihilated the English at the Battle of
Killiecrankie in 1689.

The area of the Battle of Cromdale is north from the Spey
Bridge, where the River Spey wanders like a serpent
overlooked on the eastward side by the Hills, or Haughs, of
Cromdale. The conflict was fought on the first day of May
1690. General Buchan had been despatched in the cause of the
King to lay waste the Low Country of Scotland. He arrived on
30 April at Lethendry, just south of Cromdale, where he
encamped after placing guards near the old village church. In
the meantime, Sir Thomas Livingstone, who had been
stationed at Inverness, arrived with his troops at Derraid, near
Castle Grant, on the next day as dawn was breaking. They
crossed the Spey by a ford below Dalchapple, not unobserved
by Buchan's guards at the church. Then the King's forces made
the attack before the Highlanders could either dress themselves
or prepare for action. It was scarcely a battle, more a rout.
Some of the Highland fugitives took refuge in Lethendry
Castle, near the battlefield, and were made prisoners. Others
were overtaken at Aviemore, while another detachment was
prevented from laying a siege to Loch an Eilean Castle.

The Haughs of Cromdale are a northern rocky peninsula of
the Cairngorm range and separate the River Spey from its

tributary, the Avon. Cromdale itself was originally a settlement with a church as its nucleus and was known as Kirktown of Cromdale. It was a crossing place by ferry over the Spey, which accounts for some of the rather puzzling names in the area: Nether Port, Upper Port, East Port and West Port. All these are in fact associated with the access routes to the river bank. In 1609 Cromdale was erected into 'ane free burgh and baronie' by King James VI. It had its own courthouse, prison and a hanging hill (Tom na Croiche). The decay of Cromdale as a burgh is said to have been hastened by a market-day fight between rival factions of the Clan Grant; after this incident the Laird of Grant decided to build Grantown on Spey.

The parish church of St Ma-Luac and St Bridget is situated down beside the bridge over the Spey and is sheltered by two very large trees. It was erected in 1809. Its importance for the area is seen in the large churchyard. Some of the gravestones tell stories of just how far-travelled were some of the natives from around Cromdale: India, St Vincent Island and Canada. One survivor of Waterloo is buried here.

At Bridge of Avon, the River Avon makes its contribution to the waters of the Spey, at a convergence overlooked by Ballindalloch Castle. In its heyday the castle was said to have been one of the finest specimens of the Scottish baronial style. The oldest part dates from 1546. The building was completely restored in 1850. The grounds are famous for the displays of daffodils in the spring. When the castle was first built, the masons had a sore time of it. No sooner had the walls reached a certain height, than they were knocked down again by some mysterious agency. So often did this happen that the Laird set up a watch during one night and found that towards early morning a great wind came roaring down from Ben Rinnes, which not only whirled the half-built walls into the Avon but pitched the Laird and his attendant into a holly bush. A demoniacal voice was heard to say three times: 'Build on the cow haugh'. The Laird, mindful of what might happen if he ignored the order, then caused the new castle to be built on the low ground, instead of the higher ground as he had wished. There were no further problems.

The castle has seen its share of the turbulence of Scottish history. In 1645 the Marquis of Montrose set it on fire in his

Telford's Craigellachie Bridge, August 1986. *(Photograph: Robert R F Kinghorn, from* Speyside Railways *by Rosemary A Burgess and Robert R F Kinghorn)*

lightning campaign of that year. The building is a typical Z-plan castle with a round tower to the north-west and a square one to the south-east. In 1602 a wide circular stair-tower was added, crowned by a cap-house with an attractive little oriel window. The castle and grounds are private, though they are open to the public on special occasions. What can be seen from the road is the nineteenth-century gatehouse, a Gothic turreted creation from 1850, which combines the entrance to the grounds of the castle with the old bridge over the River Avon. Both the bridge and the gatehouse, under the beeches on the steep bank of the river, are an attractive sight and can be easily visited by steps down from the new bridge, just opposite the Post Office.

The whitewashed parish church of St Peter was built in 1809. Records show, however, that this site has been a place of worship since the thirteenth century. It is prominently perched on a terrace at the foot of a steep lane leading down from the A95. An old prophecy that it will 'gang down the Spey full of folk' reminds us of the severity of the Spey in springtime when floods threaten the river banks. Three Pictish stones, with their mysterious symbols, are attached to the wall of the church, a reminder of just how ancient are the lands of Inveravon. A small mausoleum surmounts the remains of the first baronets of Ballindalloch, the Macpherson-Grants. One famous ancestor, whose tomb is in the grounds of the castle, was General James Grant (1720-1806) who fought in Flanders, at Culloden and in Wolfe's campaigns in Canada. He became Governor of Florida in 1760 before retiring to Ballindalloch.

To the east of Bridge of Avon, the prominent granite peak of Ben Rinnes, at 2755 feet, stands as a reminder, with its attendant sgurrs, of its association with the solid rock of the Grampians. From the top, one can almost number off a fair proportion of the whisky distilleries of Speyside, for this is pure malt country.

The village of Charleston of Aberlour was founded in 1812 by Charles Grant of Wester Elchies, on much the same lines as was Grantown on Spey. Feus, with four acres of land attached, were granted on liberal terms and were soon in great demand. The channel of the Spey provided some of the building materials needed for the new houses, which certain rather frugal feuars carried to the new village in hand-barrows, with the assistance of their wives.

The outstanding feature of this small burgh is the width of the main street, lined with trees. In older times, the parish was called Skirdustan, from the old church there having been dedicated to St Drostan. It was Charles Grant who offered the advice: 'It is in the interest of every gentleman possessed of ane estate in the Highlands to collect a number of Mechanicks and other industrious people into some centricall spot'. His advice was not lost on other estate-owning lairds.

Aberlour thus began its late history with the 'Mechanicks' or tradesmen congregating in the new town and setting up in business in the main street. Some years ago Aberlour suffered a drastic fall in its population, due to a peculiar circumstance: the closure of the town's famous orphanage, which provided home and upbringing for between 300 and 400 children from many parts of Scotland.

Though much of the original history has now gone, Aberlour is in the heartland of the whisky country and boasts its own distillery. Some might say that the best shortbread in

Jane Maxwell, fourth Duchess of Gordon by George Romney.
(Scottish National Portrait Gallery)

the world is made in Aberlour, the product of a small bakery
venture established in 1909. The shortbread is exported to
several overseas countries and gives much-needed work to
many people. The shortbread is based on traditional recipes
and is made by traditional methods. The ingredients are simply
flour, sugar, butter and salt made into a magical mixture by
decades of expertise.

Across the Spey, taking the turn-off from the A95 to the west, yet another well-laid-out village is Archiestown. It was established in 1760 by yet another of the Grant clan: Sir Archibald Grant of Monymusk. In 1783 the new settlement was largely destroyed by fire, but was rebuilt. Its grid system gives it a neat appearance. The 18ft-high war memorial was unveiled in 1920 by the Duke of Richmond and Gordon.

The Agricultural Museum reflects the way of life of those who once relied on the produce of the land for their life and living.

Following the route of the Spey once more, Craigellachie offers a graceful sight for the eyes: Telford's Bridge. In the early years of last century there was no bridge across the river between Fochabers and Grantown, some thirty miles inland. It was suggested by local landowners that Craigellachie would be the best site to locate such a convenience. Thomas Telford, already a bridge builder *par excellence,* was asked to design something suitable and he came up with one of the most elegant and graceful structures in the country. It was erected in 1815 for the modest price (in today's terms) of £8000. It is a prefabricated iron structure whose parts were cast hundreds of miles away at Plas Kynaston in Wales. The bridge was then brought piece by piece to the Highlands.

Telford took some good advice from the locals who recommended that the bridge be built some five feet higher than was originally intended. It was timely advice because it was only by some inches that the bridge avoided being swept away in the Moray floods of 1829 when the Spey rose by 15½ feet. Until a new bridge was constructed nearby, the old one presented a problem for traffic with its very sharp right turn below a great cliff rising straight out of the Spey.

Craigellachie itself is built on terraces above the River Spey close by where the River Fiddich feeds its tributary waters into the parent river. Essentially Victorian in character, it saw its heyday towards the end of last century when it was a great place for fresh-air holidays, to say nothing of salmon fishing. It has a distillery and two large cooperages.

From Craigellachie, the Spey winds its way northwards through low country to Rothes, passing through Arndilly, with Ben Aigan to the east. This peak used to be part of the

Fochabers Parish Church. *(Photograph: Hamish Brown)*

Arndilly estate which was, for generations, noted for its magnificent and well-managed woodlands of fir, larch, spruce and oak, which successive owners had planted with an eye to the future. Arndilly House, glimpsed from the road, was built about 150 years ago by David McDowal Grant who, in his time, was one of the great land 'improvers' in Banffshire. He devoted much of his time and money to the proper development of his estate.

Arndilly, however, is much older. Under the name of Ardendol it was the centre of its own parish as early as 1215, and came into Grant ownership when it was bought by Thomas Grant. Grant was the patron of a young lad called James Fergusson, born in Rothiemay in 1715. From humble origins the lad made progress in his education under Grant's watchful eye to become the most famous astronomer in Scotland and to be respected as a scholar in such varied disciplines as politics, history, moral philosophy and mechanical engineering.

Partly self-taught, Fergusson learned the rudiments of astronomy while looking after his sheep on the hills. Thomas Grant had the knack of attracting unusual men around him. One was Alexander Cantley, Grant's butler, of whom Fergusson was to write: 'He was the most extraordinary man that I was ever acquainted with, or perhaps I shall ever see; for he was a complete master of arithmetic, a good mathematician, a master of music on every known instrument except the harp, understood Latin, French and Greek, and let blood extremely well, and could even prescribe as a physician upon any urgent occasion'. With all that to his credit, one wonders why Cantley found the harp so difficult to play!

The village of Rothes, on the west bank of the Spey, was founded in 1766, on the site of an older settlement close by the castle of Rothes. It was basically a crofting community with no aspirations to commercial greatness until, in 1840, J. & J. Grant built a distillery to produce the famous Glen Grant whisky. Eventually Rothes could boast no fewer than five distilleries. Some witnesses to this industry are the soot-blackened gravestones in the old burial ground next to the distilleries in the town beside the Linn of Rothes.

Old Rothes Castle is now in a ruinous state with only a single massive wall remaining. It was built in the thirteenth century and was inhabited until 1622 and finally burned down about 1700 to prevent thieves using it as a base. Its stones were said to have been used by the folk of Rothes to build their houses. King Edward I spent some time in the castle in July 1296 on his way south after a punitive expedition further north.

Rothes Kirk was built in 1781 and added to in 1812, then re-built in 1868. Two years later the clock tower was added, the clock being the old town clock from Nairn – truly second hand!

Baxter's Visitors' Centre. *(Photograph: Hamish Brown)*

From Rothes, the Spey takes a few convoluted turns to the north-east to Boat of Brig. The rather curious conjunction in this name of two methods of crossing the water is due to the fact that an old bridge across the Spey at this spot fell into decay and was replaced by a ferry-boat, which came to be known as the 'boat of the bridge'. The old bridge is said to have been the first, and for many years the only, bridge that spanned the Spey. Records of its existence date from the thirteenth century.

After leaving Boat of Brig, the Spey enters the last lap of its long journey from Loch Spey; mountains are replaced by low hills and wooded plantations and the last major settlement is reached: Fochabers, on the east bank, with the palatial Gordon Castle to its north.

For centuries the whole of this district was part of the extensive estates of the Dukes of Gordon, which at one time extended all the way from the Moray Firth to Ben Nevis in Lochaber, interrupted only by a two-mile strip in Rothiemurchus which belonged to someone else. Their thousands of acres in Strathspey took in the great Forest of Glenmore. Although the income from rents, salmon fishings, grouse moors and forestry concessions was considerable, in 1785 the fourth Duke of Gordon found himself strapped for ready cash and he sold the standing timber in Glenmore Forest to William Osbourne from Hull for £70,000. As we shall see, when we arrive at Kingston, this Osbourne built a shipyard at the mouth of the Spey and set up a successful business with a partner.

The Gordons have a colourful page to themselves in Scotland's history. When Robert Burns visited Gordon Castle on his Highland Tour he wrote:

> *Wildly here without control,*
> *Nature reigns and rules the whole.*

Later, someone else was moved to write that these lines 'would be a more accurate description of the private lives of the Gordons of that time, than of the parish itself'.

Alexander, fourth Duke of Gordon, and his Duchess were quite a pair. He occupied most of his time raising regiments and companies for the British Army, while the Duchess busied herself in scheming and plotting to marry her daughters off to the richest noblemen in the country; she was not too successful. Between them, they had a staggering number of illegitimate children, apart from legally-begot offspring. Names were a problem, particularly for the two sons named George, a problem solved by the Duchess referring to them as 'the Duke's George' and 'my George'.

It was the Duke's George who succeeded to the title, but he proved no better at managing his affairs than his father. When he died, the last of his line in 1836, he owed the not inconsiderable sum of £45,000 to the bank. His titles and estates went to the Duke of Richmond, who also took the name of Gordon. When he died in 1935, the Gordon estate around Fochabers came into the possession of the Commissioners for Crown Lands, with the Forestry Commission taking over part of the estate for the Forest of Speymouth.

Gordon Castle itself is a sprawling but magnificent affair in an equally magnificent setting. The castle, founded in 1498, was almost totally rebuilt by the fourth Duke of Gordon towards the end of the eighteenth century. The gardens were

Fochabers Museum – a mock-up of a Victorian grocery shop in this fascinating museum. *(Photograph: Hamish Brown)*

laid out as extensive and pleasant policies. Some holly trees are the originals mentioned in the song 'The Blue Bells of Scotland', with the 'Highland Laddie' being the Marquis of Huntly. He accompanied Sir Richard Abercrombie to Holland in 1799 as Colonel of the 92nd Gordon Highlanders:

> *Oh, where, tell me where, is your Highland laddie gone?*
> *He's gone with streaming banners, where noble deeds are done,*
> *And my sad heart will tremble till he comes safely home.*
> *Ah, where, tell me where, did your Highland laddie stay?*
> *He dwelt beneath the holly trees, beside the rapid Spey,*
> *And mony a blessing followed him the day he went away.*

Apart from her extra-marital activities, the fourth Duke of Gordon's Duchess has gone into the pages of Scottish regimental history as the woman who raised the Gordon Highlanders with a shilling between her lips and a kiss for each recruit. As Jane Maxwell, she was one of the beauties of her day, and to have kissed the Duchess of Gordon was something many an old soldier wove into a story of his own making, to earn an extra drink or a meal in the local alehouse.

The town of Fochabers owes its origin to the removal of an older village by the fourth Duke to make room for the rebuilding of Gordon Castle, as he found it 'inconvenient' to have the settlement so near to his home. Fochabers represents the 'improving movement' of the day and is a fine example of eighteenth-century town planning, though its main street now carries the busy A96 traffic from Aberdeen to Inverness. By the end of the eighteenth century the new village had rid itself of its reputation as a 'poor place', which was how Dr Samuel Johnson described it.

The parish church, on the south side of the main square, is a well-proportioned building with a pillared portico and dignified spire. Much of the architecture of the town is the work of John Baxter, who was mason to William Adam, the renowned Scottish architect. Another of Fochabers' benefactors was Alexander Milne, who emigrated to America because he did not want to have his hair cut as the Duke required. He made a fortune in America, and when he returned to his native parish he founded Milne's High School, built in the Tudor Revival style.

The descendants of two of the Duke's retainers have been responsible for much of Fochabers' prosperity. Baxters are now world-famous for their food products. The firm's Visitor Centre is well worth a visit; it is located about a mile west of Fochabers. Not to be missed is Christie's Garden Centre, with its white peacocks and floral clock. A visit to the Fochabers Folk Museum, in Pringle Church, on the High Street will take one back to yesteryear to see some of the lifestyles of our forebears.

The museum is a witness to private enterprise and energy. It actually started with a problem: what to do with a mounting collection of old family possessions (furniture, kitchenware and lacework) and the collecting mania of the Museum Curator, Gordon Christie. When Mr Christie bought a horse-drawn gig, he was hooked and soon owned another fourteen and a hearse. When Pringle Church came up for sale, thirty years after it had seen its last service, it was the answer to a prayer, literally.

The Museum now houses much of Fochabers' history,

William Marshall, engraving by John Moir.
(Photograph: Scottish National Portrait Gallery)

including the drawings for the planned village. It contains a Victorian bedroom and a grocery shop complete with unopened provisions dating from 1952, when a nearby shop closed its doors and was left neglected for thirty years.

Bellie Churchyard lies to the north of the Gordon Castle estate, about a mile and a half north of Fochabers itself. Look out for the Saunders Stone, commemorating a man who died aged 107 years. Another stone commemorates John Menzies, for fifty years factor to the Duke of Gordon, 'who never sustained any loss by his incorrectness or neglect of duty and the many thousands with whom he transacted business were equally satisfied with the integrity of his conduct against which no complaint was ever heard even from those who were not his friends'. Praise indeed!

Before we leave Fochabers, one famous son must be given his due as a major contributor to Scotland's store of traditional music: William Marshall, buried in Bellie Churchyard and merely noted as factor to the fourth Duke of Gordon.

There are many old documents which mention the Highlanders' love of dancing and the making of music. By the seventeenth century a characteristic form of music had established itself and was attaining a popularity which it still retains, as an accompaniment to the foursome reel, possibly the most popular Highland dance there is. The strathspey is the name given to tunes played in a comparatively slow tempo; they were called 'ports' and are found written in the Skene and Stralloch manuscripts (1615-1625 and 1627-1629). They are ideally suited to the fiddle and a school of composers of this type developed in Strathspey. There is a tradition that the earliest of strathspeys was that played by James Macpherson who played his 'Macpherson's Rant' at the foot of his gallows tree in 1700. Between 1750 and 1830 the strathspey's popularity had reached its zenith and, indeed, so great was the demand for new tunes that many Strathspey fiddlers and composers moved to Edinburgh and to London to satisfy the demands of society for dancing to 'Scotch music', which was to develop the 'Scotch snap' – a short note (on the beat) followed by a long one occupying the rest of the beat. Some outstanding fiddlers now rest in the halls of fame such as Neil Gow (of Dunkeld), his son Nathaniel and, of course, William Marshall.

Marshall was born in Fochabers in 1749, into a humble but industrious household. With the exception of some six months at a grammar school, he received no education but what his father taught him. When he was twelve years of age he entered the service of the Duke of Gordon. He taught himself mechanics, astronomy, architecture and music. He was composing songs long before he was persuaded to publish them. When he eventually did so, he found it necessary to state on the front cover of his book that the contents were all his own compositions and that other people had been changing the names of some of his tunes and publishing them as their own.

The famous viaduct at Garmouth. *(Photograph: Hamish Brown)*

This warning is supposed to have been directed chiefly at the Gows, for there are two footnotes to tunes in the book stating that the Gows had appropriated the melody and changed the name. Ethical standards were not particularly high in those days as regards copyright. Marshall composed some 114 strathspey tunes. The tune 'Marquis of Huntly's Farewell' is regarded as the most beautiful strathspey ever composed. One eminent musical authority has asked 'whether with this tune, strathspey music has not said its vital last word'.

Marshall made his own instruments – cellos and fiddles – and several clocks, including a water clock, some of which survive today. One of his cellos was unearthed from an attic in the 1930s. A fiddle of his is now in New Zealand where it is still played and cherished. He died in 1833 aged 84 years.

To follow the Spey's final course to feed the waters of the Moray Firth, one takes one or other of two routes. The first is the B9104 which runs on the east bank of the river to Spey Bay and Tugnet.

Spey Bay stands among the great shingle banks that are

being continually pushed westward by longshore drift and which threaten to close the mouth of the Spey. Even in this century it has been necessary three times to cut a new channel at the river mouth. Spey Bay is now a popular holiday resort, with a hotel and an excellent eighteen-hole golf course. Anyone interested in bird life will not be disappointed, for this area teems with a wide variety of species.

Just along from Spey Bay is the tiny village of Tugnet. The name is appropriate for it is here, at the mouth of the Spey, that salmon have been caught by netting for centuries. The Ice House, the largest of its kind in Scotland, was built in 1831 as a store house for ice used to pack salmon. The building has now been restored and houses a fascinating exhibition dealing with the salmon-fishing industry and the wildlife of the Spey estuary. The Ice House is also the northern terminus of the Speyside Way.

Standing on the spit of land at Tugnet one can watch the swift-flowing Spey eager to discharge its waters into the Moray Firth, an eagerness which has created problems with the pebble barriers. The river, in fact, has now reached sea level, having fallen at the rate of twelve feet per mile since its origin in Loch Spey.

To get to the last two major settlements at the mouth of the Spey one must trek back to the village of Mosstodloch, a couple of miles west of Fochabers, and take the B9015 to reach Garmouth.

Once a fishing port, Garmouth thrived until the unruly Spey changed its route into the Moray Firth to leave it landlocked. But for all its reflective mood, Garmouth has seen some rumbustious times and has its due place in the pages of Scotland's history. It was erected into a Burgh of Barony in 1587 by King James VI. In the year 1645 the Marquis of Montrose paid two visits: in February he plundered the folk and in September he returned to burn the village, as part of the Covenanting wars which tore Scotland apart.

It was in Garmouth that King Charles II landed in 1650, returning from exile to take up the throne as a 'Covenanted King'. He signed the historic Solemn League and Covenant, an act which he performed with great reluctance because the intention was to impose Scots-style Presbyterianism on episcopal England. A plaque on the wall of a corner house in the 'Loanie' in Garmouth reminds us of the event. The honeymoon did not last. By the autumn of 1651 Scotland was overrun by Cromwellian forces and two years later was absorbed into a single British 'Commonwealth'.

On the last Saturday in June of each year is held the Maggie Fair. This is one of the few ancient Scottish fairs which still survives. It commemorates the creation of Garmouth as a burgh of barony and derives its name from Lady Margaret Kerr who married Sir James Innes and brought the Dukedom of Roxburghe into the Innes family.

Less than a mile away from Garmouth lies Kingston at the very mouth of the Spey. It owes its name to two Englishmen from Yorkshire who established shipbuilding operations there nearly two centuries ago. One of them came from Kingston-on-Hull, and what better reminder of home than to call one's new abode by the same name? For a long time Kingston comprised only a few dwellings of the salmon fishers who took advantage of the Atlantic-run salmon making for the upper reaches of the Spey to spawn. It also served as a port. In time its importance increased, particularly with the shipbuilding operations, and larger houses were built, rather foolishly, on the banks of the Spey. Until the year 1829 the river behaved itself and the mouth of the estuary was stable. But that year saw the great Spey floods which swept away many of Kingston's houses; some of the present-day buildings were erected from rubble from their ruins.

The oldest building in Kingston predates the shipyards by several centuries: Dunfermline House, known originally as Red Corff House, this name meaning that it was used for the curing of salmon and the storing of the nets. The lower part of the building is believed to have been erected as a changing-house by the monks of Dunfermline Abbey, who manned the Priory of Urquhart. The upper storey was added about 1780 and the house became the headquarters of a flourishing shipyard business. The house has since been restored as a private dwelling and is not open to the public. It can be seen by the road at the entrance to the village.

Today Kingston is a peaceful village with no trace of its former busy times, when ships were launched to trade all over the world. One line of cottages on Beach Road has back gardens virtually bordering the Spey, almost tempting fate. But, so far, the river simply flows through the shingle spits and estuarine islands teeming with bird life.

CHAPTER 7

Tributary Waters

While the River Spey may take all the credit for its journey through Strathspey from the headwaters of Loch Spey, its fame is in no small measure due to the waters from other rivers. Some of these are of considerable length and volume and most have an interesting history of their own. It would thus be an injustice if one were to ignore the significant contributions which these rivers have made. More often than not, these tributaries of the Spey find their headwaters high up in the Cairngorms, although the impetuous Dulnain has its source in the western heights of the Monadhliath Mountains.

One of the most southerly tributaries is the River Truim, which begins with its headwaters in Drumochter and flows north-west to join the Spey at Invertruim. Its birthplace is the Sow of Atholl and the Boar of Badenoch, fitting names for a river which finds its way into the Spey Valley. The Truim rises on the old Inverness-shire/Perthshire boundary on An Torc, about 2500 feet above sea level. It then takes a northward course of some fifteen miles to meet the Spey. Its route runs almost parallel with the main road and rail links into the Highlands. The Truim has a contribution from the waters of Allt Cuiaich, a stream which has its main source in Loch na Cuiaich on the slopes of Meall na Cuiaich (3120 feet), a prominent round-topped hill seen from many parts of Badenoch. Glen Truim itself tends to be rather monotonous and desolate, the scene being relieved only when the land falls away and the lower hills present a more varied vegetation.

The Falls of Truim, just south of Etteridge, present an attractive sight and are easily reached from the main road. At times of low water, however, the Falls give salmon no end of trouble as they try to negotiate their way upriver to spawn. The bridge at Crubenmore, now some 200 years old, once carried the A9 roadway from Perth to Inverness until it was replaced in 1928 by a concrete structure. The old bridge began to deteriorate and it was in danger of collapse some years ago.

But a rescue operation was mounted and it has now been restored to something of its former glory. All the work was carried out by volunteers, spurred on by the Scottish Rights of Way Society. What was interesting about the volunteers was that the young lads who worked on the project were from Polmont Conservation Corps in the Polmont Borstal Institution. The actual date of the erection of Crubenmore Bridge is not certain; it has been thought that it was built after the period when General Wade and his successors built their main roads and bridges, a period which ended in 1780. A picnic facility has been installed to allow sightseers to enjoy the scenery.

To the west of the Truim, a smaller stream called Mashie Water, ten miles long, rises on Meall Cruaidh, a hill on the west side of Loch Ericht. For the most part, the Mashie runs through wooded land before it joins the Spey to the west of Laggan Bridge. The waters of the river are taken into the conduit of the North of Scotland Hydro-Electric Board near Strathmashie House, whence it is piped westwards to feed the River Pattack and then emptied into Loch Laggan. Strath Mashie is one of the shortest straths in the Highlands.

The River Tromie, about twenty miles long, rises on the borders of Perthshire. It has two principal headstreams, Amhainn Gharbh Ghaig and Allt na Craoibhe, which combine to form Loch an t-Seilich, from which issues the Tromie. Glen Tromie is a breeding area for the scarce twite. A footpath from Blair Atholl takes one through to Kingussie. This is in fact a very old route to the north and is the only road northwards shown on Green's map of 1689 and Moll's map of 1725.

It was superseded by the military road over the Drumochter Pass constructed by General Wade in 1728-30, although after that date the Minigaig Pass still appeared on maps as a 'summer road to Ruthven'. The route is about twenty-eight miles from Kingussie to Blair Atholl and has some of the most interesting scenery in the Highlands, to say nothing of an abundance of wildlife.

Glen Tromie itself is a wild and lonely glen. Alders and birches clothe the rocky banks of the lower portion of the glen which offer some cover for a number of small birds. On the east side of the glen is a hill named Croidh-la, across the face of which is a large and unusual rock formation. This is best seen

The Falls of Truim, Glen Truim, where in autumn salmon can often be seen leaping the Falls on their way upstream to spawn. *(Photograph: David Gowans)*

from Kingussie (on a clear day!) some five miles away and presents something like the shape of a horse facing south.

To the east of Glen Tromie is Glen Feshie and its attendant river, the Feshie, which discharges its waters into the Spey just north of Loch Insh and Kincraig after a journey of some twenty-two miles. The Feshie's headwaters are on the borders of Perthshire, on Leathad an Tobhain (2994 feet). The river is fed by dozens of mountain streams, some of which are of particular significance with spectacular waterfalls.

Glen Feshie has many associations with both history and personalities. It was at one time among the most important deer forests in the Highlands and as such it attracted the hunting fraternity last century. The man who might be called the father of Speyside tourism, Sir Edwin Landseer, haunted the locality around the confluence of the Feshie and Allt Coire Bhlair to make the sketches for his famous paintings. The most famous of all, 'The Monarch of the Glen', sums up his affinity with the area. One of the waterfalls on the Feshie was made the subject of a painting and is now known as Landseer's Falls; it is over 130ft high. The high rise in this area, Sron Ban-righ, is associated with a traditional tale about the burning of the old forest hereabouts. Mary, Queen of Scots, was hunting in the district and was offended by her husband who, returning from a distant hunting expedition, asked about the state of the forests rather than enquiring as to his wife's welfare. At this slight she gave orders to set the forests on fire, and watched the conflagration from the summit of Sron Ban-righ.

The Feshie River's most important tributary is the River Eidart which has a fine waterfall near to its junction with the Feshie. It has been noted by geologists that the upper course of the Feshie presents an excellent example of the shifting of a watershed and the capture of the headwaters of a stream belonging to another river system.

The Eidart, which joins the Feshie about a mile below the point where the latter river touches the boundary between Aberdeenshire and Inverness-shire, was once the headstream of that river; but the Feshie has gradually cut back its bed to the march between the two counties and captured the upper part of the River Geldie. Thus, the former headwaters are now those of the Feshie, and the watershed between the basins of

The restored Wade bridge at Crubenmore, Glen Truim.
(Photograph: Hamish Brown)

the Rivers Spey and Dee has been shifted more than six miles eastwards.

No less a personage than Queen Victoria passed through Glen Feshie: twice, in 1860 and in 1861. She wrote in her Journal (1860): 'The Feshie and the Geldie rise almost on a level, with very little distance between them. The Feshie is a fine rapid stream full of stones. As you approach the glen, which is very narrow, the scenery becomes very fine – particularly after fording the Etchart (Eidart), a very deep ford . . . Then we came upon a most lovely spot – the scene of Landseer's glory – and where there is a little encampment of wooden and turf huts, built by the late Duchess of Bedford . . . We were quite enchanted with the beauty of the view'.

In 1861 she trekked through the glen again: 'Brown waded through the Etchart leading my pony; and then two of the others, who were riding on another pony, dropped the whole bundle of cloaks in the water! . . . I felt what a delightful little encampment it [the huts] must have been, and how enchanting to live in such a spot as this solitary wood in a glen surrounded by the high hills. We got off, and went into one of the huts to look at a fresco of stags of Landseer's over a chimney piece'.

For nearly two centuries Glen Feshie has been the target for proposals to build a new route into the Highlands. A road through the glen was first mooted by General Wade in the first half of the eighteenth century, but he dropped the idea in favour of more logical routes to link north and south. In 1828 engineers Thomas Telford and Joseph Mitchell surveyed the route through the glen in their capacity as agents for the Commissioners for Highland Roads and Bridges. The glen was considered as a suitable alternative to the long detour through the Drumochter Pass to get from Perth to Inverness. But the high altitude of the watersheds and the ever-present danger from snow led to the plan being abandoned. The idea, however, still retained some residual heat.

During the Second World War the glen suffered much from the uncompromising needs of hostilities. Many of the old pines, which had stood for centuries, were felled by soldiers; lumber camps were set up, roads were driven up the hillsides and the salmon were dynamited in the rivers.

Towards the end of 1972 the proposal for a road through Glen Feshie was aired again, this time to link Aberdeenshire and Inverness-shire. The thinking this time was that increased tourist traffic would produce the necessary incentive for central Government to come up with the cash. Certainly, such a road facility would offer a convenient link between the winter sports area in the Cairngorms and Glen Shee and Beinn a' Bhuird. Only time will tell whether this magnificent glen, even in its damaged state, will become yet another sacrifice on the altar of progress.

The source of the River Druie is Loch Einich below the beetling height of Sgoran Dubh Mor (3635ft). The loch is cradled in the arms of a circle of high peaks. The river actually picks up its name from the Allt Druidh at the mouth of the pass known as the Lairig Ghru, one of the ancient rights of way in the Cairngorms from Speyside to Braemar. The Pass is about 17 miles long and it takes up to twelve hours of hard trekking to go from end to end, keeping to a well-trodden path marked by cairns on the higher reaches.

The River Luineag feeds its own waters into the Druie at Coylumbridge. This river has its source in Loch Morlich in Glenmore Forest Park.

Proof that one can have a taste of both worlds in Strathspey. Away from the many outdoor activities which the Aviemore area offers, one can spend a day or two simply trekking through the quiet and almost secret places among the birches and pines of Speyside. The Cairngorms are, however, never far away, with the gap of the Lairig Ghru in the far distance (left). *(Courtesy Scottish Tourist Board)*

On the south-eastern side of Cairngorm lies Loch Avon, the source of the River Avon, which runs for 38 miles and is the longest, as well as being the most important, tributary of the Spey, whose waters it enters at Ballindalloch. It is also the fastest-flowing river in Scotland. Loch Avon rests in a deep valley dating from the glacial period and is fed by streams of truly high birth: from Cairngorm, Ben Macdhui and Beinn Mheadoin. The river flows in an easterly direction until it takes a sharp turn northwards at Inchrory, which has always been something of a crossroads. It was the meeting place of the old cattle drove roads from the north via the Avon to Braemar and Donside. As such it was also a good bottleneck for the reiving or cattle-raiding traffic which was a common activity in the seventeenth and eighteenth centuries, a fact which did not escape the attention of General Wade. Between 1747 and 1750 military patrols were stationed at Inchrory and were successful in intercepting cattle thieves.

The sharp elbow bend of the River Avon at Inchrory is due to the original glacial action from ice sheets which once covered the north of Scotland. Geologists have suggested that the Avon was the original source of the River Don which now flows to Aberdeen; but the Avon was severed from the Don by the pressure of ice flowing in the direction of Tomintoul.

Before the Avon enters Strathavon it passes the village of Tomintoul, one of the highest villages in the Highlands (1150ft above sea level). It was founded in 1776 by the fourth Duke of Gordon but never succeeded in establishing itself as a centre for anything other than a crofting community. Even so, it had some pretensions: by the 1820s there were three inns in the village square. However, when Queen Victoria passed through it in 1860 she described Tomintoul as '. . . the most tumble-down, poor-looking place I ever saw – a long street with three inns, miserable dirty-looking houses and people, and a sad look of wretchedness about it'.

Things are much better now. It has a trim square, flanked by trees, at the centre of which is a now-dry drinking fountain with an invitation on its iron steps: 'Bairns, step up'. The village is laid out in a grid-iron pattern with the main street about one mile long. Tomintoul serves the tourist industry well, particularly since the development of the ski-tows at the Lecht. On the third Saturday of each July the Tomintoul Games are held. Established as long ago as 1824, the Games attract many national and international 'stars' in the so-called heavy events, such as putting the shot and tossing the caber.

In common with most communities hereabouts, the past has been revived, not only to remind the older generation of how change has affected their lives, but also to inform the younger generation about their roots. Tomintoul Museum, in the Square, does this job admirably. It contains a reconstructed rural kitchen and blacksmith's shop. It also includes much historical information about Tomintoul and the surrounding area.

A piece of interesting British military history lies up the A939 road out of Tomintoul to Ballater through the Lecht. About a half-mile beyond Blairmarrow, just over a small bridge, is a ruined cottage known as Toplis' Cottage. This house, for a few days in 1920, featured in the national Press as

A quiet corner of the square, Tomintoul, the highest town in the Highlands. *(Photograph: Hamish Brown)*

the hiding place of Percy Toplis, whose exploits as a confidence trickster in the First World War were written up in *The Monocled Mutineer* and featured on television.

As though his deeds of daring and impersonation during the War were not enough, he was also a prime suspect in the murder of a taxi driver near Andover in Kent. Toplis headed north to escape the heat. He cycled most of the way to the Lecht where he laid up. He might have continued undetected for a long time had he not started to break up the furniture in the cottage to start a fire, which attracted the attention of the farmer at Blairmarrow. The Tomintoul 'bobby' was called and the two men approached the cottage. There they were met by Toplis with a loaded revolver which he fired, slightly wounding both men. Toplis then escaped on his bicycle and headed over the Lecht. He got as far as Penrith in Cumberland where he was identified and shot as a dangerous criminal. Some folk in Tomintoul still remember him, a memory reinforced by a faded unpaid bill for repairs to his bicycle.

The River Livet joins the Avon at Drumin. The ruined castle at Drumin is now little more than two-and-a-bit walls and the structure is in such bad condition that it is out of bounds in the interests of public safety. The castle was once one of the strongholds of the infamous 'Wolf of Badenoch' who burnt Elgin Cathedral in 1390.

Glenlivet itself now rests securely in the litany of malt whisky names and the 'Glenlivet' distillery is one of the stops on the Whisky Trail. A well-organised Visitors' Centre in the village of Glenlivet displays the process of whisky-making and offers a welcoming dram. On show is a reconstruction of Landseer's painting 'The Illicit Still' showing a smuggler and his family, a slaughtered stag, no doubt poached for the pot, and the copper worm which distilled the amber liquid.

As in the days of the whisky smuggler, the waters of the River Livet still supply a number of distilleries. At one time it was recorded that no fewer than 200 illicit stills were in operation in this district, a situation which the excisemen had a hard time to cope with, until the Glenlivet distillery became legal and operated so successfully that it gave the lead to others to follow the process of legitimisation.

The area of the Braes of Glenlivet was once the site of the only post-Reformation Roman Catholic college in Scotland, based at Scalan, on the Crombie Water, a tributary of the Livet. It was a modest turf-covered building and served its students well until 1726 when the students were dispersed by the military; but it was re-opened the following year. Then came a period of harassment. In 1746 the Duke of Cumberland sent a detachment of soldiers to burn the place down, with the students fleeing to the hills for safety. Another building was erected, to be abandoned in 1799 for a new site at Aquhorties near Inverurie which, in its turn, gave place to Blairs College near Aberdeen.

The remains of the earlier building can be seen on the near side of the Crombie Water, just above the Bishop's Well, which is still in use and valued for its sweet-tasting clean water.

But for a geological circumstance, the River Nethy might have laid a claim to Loch Avon as its source. Instead, it has at present to be content with its origin on the Saddle of Cairngorm, less than a mile to the north side of Loch Avon. It has a good run of some fourteen miles to Nethy Bridge, through Strath Nethy and the Abernethy Forest to enter the

Dufftown, looking up Conval Street beyond the Clock Tower.
(Photograph: Hamish Brown)

Spey a little above Coulnakyle. This village has a continuous
history going back 600 years. In the thirteenth century Edward
I of England is said to have flaunted his banners at the place;
and later the noisy troops of Claverhouse pitched their tents
here. Both General MacKay and the Marquis of Montrose
made Coulnakyle their base. The old Chiefs of Grant lived at
Coulnakyle and the Baron Baillies, of the bad old days, held
their courts here to administer their rough justice. Coulnakyle
was also the headquarters of the managers of the old York
Buildings Company during the time they felled much of
Abernethy Forest.

The River Fiddich, another name closely associated with the
whisky distilling industry, is the most northerly tributary of the

Spey. It rises on the south-eastern slope of Corriehabbie Hill at an altitude of over 2300ft and lying at the head of Glen Fiddich. After a run of eighteen miles it enters the Spey at Craigellachie.

The Fiddich passes the town of Dufftown where it joins up with the Dullan Water. Dufftown was founded in 1817 by James Duff, fourth Earl of Fife, hence its name. It was originally called Balvenie, after the nearby castle of the same name. The castle itself dates from the thirteenth century and once housed Edward I of England. Mary, Queen of Scots spent some time in it on her northern campaign against the Gordon family. The castle offered refuge to the Marquis of Montrose in 1644. After the Battle of Killiecrankie in 1689, it was occupied by Jacobites and later taken over by government forces in 1746. Despite its age and its turbulent history, Balvenie Castle is in a remarkable state of preservation. It was in its time one of the largest castles in the north of Scotland.

Almost from the beginning of its existence, Dufftown was a centre of the whisky trade. Seven malt distilleries were founded here before the end of the nineteenth century and they are still flourishing today. One, Mortlach, is among the oldest in Scotland. It was founded by George Gordon and James Findlater who took out a licence in 1823, the year of the Act of Parliament which legalised the trade.

In Dufftown Town Square is the Tower which served for many years as a jail; it then acted as the Burgh Chambers and is now a museum containing material of local interest. The Clock Tower, completed in 1839, houses 'the clock that hung Macpherson'. It originally told the time to the folk of Banff and is reputed to be the clock whose hands were moved forward one hour to prevent James Macpherson, the freebooter, from gaining his reprieve from hanging.

Just outside Dufftown is Mortlach Church standing on a site which has witnessed continuous religious worship since St Moluag founded his cell here in AD 566. An interesting relic linking these early times is the 'Elephant Stone' in the church vestibule, a carved Pictish stone with an animal which looks very much like an elephant. The site is one of the oldest places of Christian worship in Scotland. In the year 1010 Malcolm III, King of Scots, extended the original building to 'three

Balvenie Castle, Dufftown. *(Photograph: Hamish Brown)*

spearlengths' in gratitude for a victory he achieved over the invading Danes after a battle which took place in the valley of the Dullan Water. The present building dates from before the Reformation but was later renovated and enlarged at various times. One of its fine stained-glass windows is in memory of Lord Stephen, a Dufftown lad who made his fortune in Canada. Born in 1829, he was apprenticed to a draper and then, after working in Aberdeen, Glasgow and London, he emigrated to Montreal where he eventually became President of the Bank of Montreal. He was later to join his cousin, Lord Strathcona, in the financing of the Canadian Pacific Railway.

To the south of Dufftown is the rise of Meikle Conval (1867ft) on whose summit, in the old days of whisky smuggling, the folk of Dufftown used to light fires to warn distillers in Glen Rinnes that the excisemen has just passed through.

About a mile and a half south-east of Dufftown is Auchindoun Castle, with its keep, some three storeys high, encircled by Pictish earthworks. Dating from the thirteenth century, it is now in an unsafe condition and is not open to the public. It was burned in 1592 during a feud between the Gordons and the Mackintoshes. Even in its ruinous state the

Dufftown golf course with its fine Highland setting.
(Photograph: Hamish Brown)

castle has an impressive air of authority and easily takes the
imagination back through the centuries to the more troubled
and dangerous times of yesteryear.

Dufftown Golf Course is reputed to have one hole which is at
a higher altitude than any other in Britain, above the 1000 ft
contour.

The only major tributary with a source to the west of the
Spey is the River Dulnain. It begins life on Beinn Breac, some
2200 ft above sea level, in the Monadhliath Mountains. It
immediately collects the waters from a number of streams
before it takes its name from Carn Dulnan, a rise on its eastern
bank. Its impetuous journey is through wild and hilly country,
sparse and monotonous, until it reaches Inverlaidnan and then
Carrbridge, when it flows through flat land which has had to
be embanked to reduce the effects of flooding. It then enters
the Spey at Dulnain Bridge.

It is a particularly swift-flowing river, rising fast after heavy
rain, and is always peat-stained. At one time it was renowned
for its salmon. An old account reads: 'There comes no salmon

in this river, but extraordinary much kipper, which are in abundance, that a gentleman thinks nothing to kill 160 in a night. They used to feast the Sheriff, and so escape the fine, but the Commonalty pay some little thing'. The 'kipper' here means salmon near or at the time of spawning.

The only other western tributary of the Spey, of minor importance, is the River Calder, which flows through Glen Banchor, the scene of some clearances last century.

CHAPTER 8

The Cairngorms

There are two ways to enjoy the Cairngorms. The first is driving into Strathspey, from either north or south, and watching the largest landmass above 3000 feet in the British Isles slowly dominate the sky. As the poet Thomas Campbell had it: 'Distance lends enchantment to the view'. And certainly this is the case when, on a bright and clear day, Cairngorm, Ben Macdhui, Carntoul and Braeriach loom large to challenge the broad plateau of the Monadhliath Mountains to the east of the River Spey. Truly, no river in Britain has such magnificent companions as it travels on its route to add its fresh waters to the salt sea of the Moray Firth.

However . . . to savour the true spirit of any landscape it is necessary to gain the peaks and survey the prospect, reflecting on man's minuscule scale in a setting where Nature is so dominant. The broad high plateau of the Cairngorms offers the promise of another world where even life itself is a rarity and those who gain access to these high places are mere temporary visitors, whether birds, animals or man.

What one sees when viewing the Cairngorms is the product of a process which occurred from 750 to 500 million years ago: what the geologists call the Caledonian 'Orogeny', or mountain-building period. During this process, when the earth was nothing but a liquid mass in space, the rock-forming fluid was belched up from the molten material deep in the earth's crust and then gradually cooled.

But the process was not so simple as a pot boiling over to leave crusts of solid material. The process also involved the mixing of ingredients which were later to become minerals, and the folding-in of materials over a basic stratum of rock, much like the folding-in of flour when baking. The Grampian range, of which the Cairngorms and the Monadhliaths form a part, consists of a succession of sedimentary sandstone, shales and limestone, deposited on a basic rock known as Lewisian gneiss, which is reckoned to be as old as 2600 million years in places.

116

Lochan Uainc in the Ryvoan Pass, Cairngorms.
(Photograph: Hamish Brown)

Through time, on a scale that is quite beyond the human imagination, much of this sediment was removed by erosion from weathering and the slow but sure working of rain, rivers, snow and ice. The 'roots' of these mountain masses lie as granitic rock known as 'plutons'. Geology is not without its romantic side, despite its highly technical nature. The name is derived from Pluto the god of the inferior regions, and is applied to igneous rocks found at some depth beneath the surface of the land or sea, as distinct from volcanic rocks, or those thrown up by volcanic action and consolidated on the surface as they cooled. The plutonic rocks are more crystalline in nature, a characteristic apparently induced by the greater pressure under which they cooled and consolidated. The Cairngorms have several of these exposed tooth-roots and parts of others which are connected to the underlying rock base.

The two main varieties of material which form the plutonic masses are granite and diorite. The former consists mainly of minerals such as potash-feldspar and quartz with some mica. The quartz, a beautiful rock, has a high silica content, and it is this which places granite in the family of acid-bearing igneous rocks, an important factor in whisky-making owing to its water-softening effect. As a mineral, quartz is properly colourless; but it does appear in coloured forms, in various shades of white, yellow, red and blue. Those who have admired the in-depth beauty of the violet-blue amethyst, the rose-quartz and the stone known as cairngorm (brown or cinnamon-yellow) will appreciate that Nature has done her work well.

Diorite, a variety of greenstone, is composed of hornblende and feldspar. It has little free quartz, but is, in contrast, commonly speckled with many black shiny mineral grains. In some parts of the Cairngorms, crystals of feldspar can be found embedded in a ground-mass of smaller-grained crystals. Fresh diorite has a pinkish colouring without many dark minerals, whereas older diorite tends to be dull-looking.

For a long time now the Cairngorms have been well known as a happy hunting ground for those who collect semi-precious stones. These are mainly associated with granite in which constituent minerals tend to be so tightly packed together that they do not develop good crystal forms. However, in places where cavities have formed as gas bubbles and where watery residual fluids have managed to enter, the minerals grow freely in crystalline form. Many large specimens of quartz, or rock crystals, have been found. Where the crystal is tinted with impurities, various shades occur, from smoky yellow to dark smoky brown: the semi-precious Cairngorm stones which are much sought after.

At one time, much treasure could be found easily on Cairngorm and on Ben Avon, but over the years commercial collecting has virtually removed all the good and accessible material. Nowadays the best localities are rightly kept a close secret. Even so, the eagle eye of the amateur gemmologist can often pick up some good crystals. These discoveries add not only excitement but pleasure to a sojourn in the Cairngorms.

Much of Cairngorm is granite and is in fact one of the largest plutonic masses in the Highlands. Its formation is still a bit of a puzzle to geologists. In the normal manner of formation of these plutons, only one or two granite peaks should be seen; yet the whole massif is a homogenous granite lump with little intrusion of diorite.

The highest peaks of the Cairngorms are over 4000 feet. They are Ben Macdhui (4296 ft), Braeriach (4248 ft), Cairntoul (4241 ft) and Cairngorm (4084 ft). These look over a lower plateau surface rising to about 2000 feet. Incisions into the plateau appear as glacially over-deepened valleys, such as those at Glen Muick and Loch Avon, with some sheer-walled corries which often contain mountain tarns.

The shape of these peaks as we see them today is the product of rain, sun and ice: Nature's agents used to ease the harshness of the original mountain-building process. Some 50 million years ago, a time far beyond the comprehension of short-lived man, the land area of what is now the Highlands was subject to the smoothing process of massive ice-sheets which covered all of Scotland. These sheets moved outwards from the highest ground to what is now the Scottish seaboard. Evidence of ice action is most easily recognised in the Highlands; it smoothed the original roughness of the rocky peaks and accentuated the existing relief.

Over great parts of the granite expanse of the Cairngorms, for instance, the ice left areas of bedrock exposed to the subsequent slow weathering which can be seen today on the high peaks. Hard rocks, however, tend to retain their original contours while their softer neighbours erode more rapidly. Glaciers blanketed much low-lying ground with a layer of sand, rubble and rock debris; their slow movement, too, gouged out many of Scotland's present-day lochs.

All the high peaks of the Cairngorms are accessible, though it is as well to stress here the need for proper clothing and careful planning before going on to the mountains. Weather conditions in particular can change quite rapidly. Specific mountain weather forecasts should always be obtained before setting out; those on radio or TV are of no use whatsoever for hill-climbing and going onto the Cairngorm plateau. Both gales and snowstorms have been recorded for every month of the

year and air frost occurs on average nearly 200 days in each
year. The Cairngorm Day Lodge has a weather monitor
(Mountainline 0479 811000) which gives updated information
on temperature, wind speeds and wind direction every thirty
minutes.

Of all the Cairngorm high peaks, Cairngorm is the most
visited because of the chairlifts and ski-tows. The top of
Cairngorm is within easy walking distance of the Ptarmigan
Observation Snack Bar. The views to all cardinal points of the
compass are magnificent. Given a clear day, the sheen on the
North Sea can be glimpsed, as can the Cuillins on Skye to the
far west. One of the problems of Cairngorm's popularity is its
very accessibility, which tends to detract from the solitary
experience one expects on a mountain top. These days on a
walk from Cairngorm to, say, Ben Macdhui one can encounter
upwards of two hundred people during the day; this compared
with perhaps less than a dozen folk on Braeriach.

This very popularity has its attendant problems, the worst
being litter. In 1972 a group of volunteers removed a quarter
of a ton of debris from the Shelter Stone and nearly two
hundredweights of broken glass from Ben Macdhui. On a visit
in 1988 the writer saw odds and ends lying about, including
plastic bottles, papers of all kinds, cellophane wrappings, crisp
bags and rusting tins. It is often said in fun, though there is a
serious point to it, that if one is short of a glove or hat, one will
find a spare one lying around on the summit of Cairngorm.

What suffers, of course, is the vegetation. To many, any
green on the ground is just grass. But the fact of the matter is
that the 'green' is composed of tiny plants which have a hard
enough time of it to survive the arctic conditions without
having to cope with often irrecoverable damage by boots. Often
people stray off the beaten tracks and mark out new routes.
Particularly on Cairngorm, treading and other damage has
reduced the plant covering and increased soil erosion.

As with the other high peaks of the Cairngorms, Cairngorm
itself offers some spectacular sights. Coire an Lochain, to the
south-west of the summit, lies below a massive slab of red
granite which in wintertime produces avalanches. Looking west
from the cliff top one can see an astonishing crack called
Savage Slit which cuts itself into the western buttress for 350

Corrour Bothy in the Lairig Ghru, Cairngorms.
(Photograph: Hamish Brown)

feet. The ridge known as Fiacaill between Coire an Lochain and Coire an t-Sneachda, is a favourite with hill walkers.

Ben Macdhui, the second highest peak in Britain, affords no less spectacular views. In 1887, the year of Queen Victoria's Golden Jubilee, a group of six climbers made it to the summit to get a sight of the bonfires which had been lit in Strathspey to celebrate the occasion. They took with them a big box of fireworks which they set off. Their show was seen by fellow climbers celebrating in their own fashion on top of Lochnagar some 18 miles away. The following morning, 23 June, the group gathered at the Shelter Stone near the grand glacial trench of Loch Avon and pledged themselves to form The Cairngorm Club: 'To open our ranks to the admission of men and women of heroic spirit, and possessed of souls open to the influences and enjoyment of nature pure and simple as displayed amongst our loftiest mountains'. As Honorary President they chose the then Liberal Member of Parliament for South Aberdeenshire, Viscount Bryce of Dechmount, who throughout his life pushed for an Access to Mountains Bill. The Cairngorm Club has done much to promote an intelligent interest in the Cairngorms and was instrumental in the rebuilding of Corrour Bothy, which was in danger of collapse.

The summit indicator on top of Ben Macdhui commemorates one of the Honorary Presidents of the Club: James Parker. The Club hut is at Muir of Inverey on the Dee side of the Cairngorms. Before the present footbridge across the Dee, near Corrour Bothy, was erected by the Club, the river had to be crossed by walking on one rope while grabbing another rope at chest height, a rather hazardous journey above the tumbling waters and their rocky bed.

For the climber and mountaineer, Ben Macdhui offers a wide variety of climbs, from easy scree shoots to a few very severe routes on the steep (400 ft) wall of Grey Man's Crag. Another wall of equal height is Creagan a' Choire Etchachan to the north-east of the Ben's summit. It is composed of hard granite jutting out in a convex shape. The Ben has a reputation for electrical storms. On one day in 1965 near the summit 50 cloud-to-earth discharges were observed, an indication of the danger which is associated with high mountain tops. The advice that in weather conditions which generate lightning, it is best to keep away from the summits or high ridges is well taken.

Over to the west from Ben Macdhui is Braeriach. The Garbh Coire of this peak is a complex system of four corries with miles of rock and vast snowfields. Garbh Choire Mor carries the most permanent snow patch in Britain. Another snowy corrie is Garbh Choire Dhaidh, with the 500-ft Dee waterfall and a high 450-ft wall of granite north of the falls. Coire Brochain is typical of the Swiss Alps with cliffs reaching over 750 feet. Compared with the human traffic on Cairngorm, very few people are seen on Braeriach.

Cairntoul a little to the south, midway between Ben Macdhui and Braeriach, broods over Lochan Uaine, a beautiful example of a high mountain tarn in arctic surroundings, and spectacular in its situation. Cairntoul tends to be ignored by experienced mountaineers because of the lack of challenging rock climbs.

While the high peaks of the Cairngorms may be the most eye-catching features of the Cairngorms, there are many lesser peaks which lend not a little interest to the panorama of the area. The miles of rock which ring Loch Avon, for instance, are regarded as the best example of natural 'wilderness' in Britain.

Broken cliffs, gigantic slabs and screes all add a new meaning to the phrase 'Nature in the raw'.

Not all the superlatives belong to the Cairngorm mountains. One of the most enjoyable walks through the Cairngorms is the 17-mile long pass called the Lairig Ghru. It is a walk, however, which must not be taken lightly. People have died in the Lairig. And the fact that the pass rises to 2733 feet as it makes it way through the mountains and corries indicates that beauty also has danger as a companion.

When viewed, say, from the A9 just north of Aviemore, the Lairig Ghru is seen as a large black gash, in the form of a rounded 'V' in the mountain plateau of Braeriach and Ben Macdhui. This is an ancient right of way much used by the folk of upper Strathspey and Mar on the Dee side of the Cairngorms. In the old days, sheep and cattle were driven through the pass, taking much longer than the ten to twelve hours needed by fit and healthy trekkers.

The path into the Lairig Ghru begins at Coylumbridge through the woods which lend some atmosphere of mystery to the journey. One might just catch a glimpse of two legendary figures associated with these woods. One, Bodach Cleocain Dearg (Old Man of the Little Red Cloak), lived at Coylumbridge. The other, Bodah Lanh-dhear (Red-handed Old Man), haunted the Loch Morlich area. What these two characters did in their own time, if they ever existed, Strathspey folklore does not tell us.

Near the entrance to the pass, the path goes by the Sinclair Memorial Hut, which dates from 1957 and commemorates Lt Col W. Sinclair who died in the Cairngorms in December 1954. A little farther on, to the left, is Lurcher's Crag (Creag an Leth-choin), a name which commemorates a great deer hunt during which a dog fell over a crag. Proposed expansion of skiing facilities has turned Lurcher's Gully into a battleground between developers and conservationists. Just before the Pools of Dee the track passes Allt na Criche, the March Burn, which plunges from the plateau and disappears underground below some boulders. The water emerges again as one large lochan and three smaller ones, all of which contain trout.

Further on, to the right, is the magnificent Coire Brochain, the corrie of gruel or porridge, a name supposedly derived from the times when cattle falling over the cliffs landed with such a thump that their bodies had the consistency of porridge. The other corrie of Braeriach (Am Braigh Riabhach, the brindled hill) is An Garbh Coire, acknowledged by many to be one of the most impressive in Scotland. Passing under the beetling brow of Ben Macdhui, the Clach an Taillear is reached, the Stone of the Tailors, a welcome chance to stop and look around to survey the scene. This massive table of rock is associated with a Strathspey story. One Hogmanay three tailors from Abernethy were celebrating the season with generous quantities of whisky, when they decided to dance at Abernethy, Rothiemurchus and Braemar, all within twenty-four hours. They started at the dell (meadow) of Abernethy first, then headed for the dell at Rothiemurchus where they spent a convivial couple of hours. Then they set out for Braemar through the Lairig Ghru, making for Dalmore, near the site of Mar Lodge on the Dee side of the Cairngorms. But they only got as far as Clach an Tailleir where they were overtaken by a blizzard and died while sheltering in the lee of the stone which now bears their name.

A little past the Tailors' Stone the Corrour Bothy can be seen, below the Devil's Point. The Bothy is over a century old but has been much altered since it was first erected. Its comforts are basic and simple, but affords welcome shelter when the weather turns sour. It was originally used as a base for deer watchers in the later Victorian and Edwardian heyday of deershooting. The Lairig Ghru track then divides; that to the left goes through Glen Luibeg, while the other track leads to Glen Dee. The eastern end of Glen Luibeg is marked by the burnt-out shell of Derry Lodge before the path enters Glen Lui and onwards to Braemar some eight miles farther on.

It must be stressed that the Lairig Ghru walk presents some tough going at times, particularly from Sinclair's Hut to the top of the pass. The route is over the top of glacial debris laid down during successive melts; and the gravel beds do not make walking easy. The path goes uphill gently but often one must change course to avoid the largest boulders. But the various resting points compensate for the difficulties encountered.

One cannot leave the Cairngorms without mentioning the legendary phantom, the Big Grey Man of Ben Macdhui, who has, for over half a century, generated a massive amount of controversial correspondence in the Scottish Press. The phenomenon dates as far back as the early nineteenth century, to James Hogg, the Ettrick Shepherd, who celebrated the brocken in verse. Over the years the stories have been amplified, coloured and exaggerated. The basis of the brocken or spectre is the shadow of someone thrown by a low sun against an opaque wall of mist, with the shadow being magnified many times and distorted by currents of wind. There are also tales of climbers, walking through crisp snow, being 'followed' by footsteps. When they stop, the footsteps also stop. But there is rather more to the simple explanations. People have told of hearing talking, laughing and even a kind of celestial music. Many have experienced psychic impressions, perhaps triggered off by an imagination intoxicated by the high mountain air. Could it be that the intense sense of loneliness, tiny man among the massive peaks of the Cairngorms, generates in the mind a pressing desire for companionship, which then manifests itself in a spiritual paraclete to walk with one through the rarefied mountain air? Mountaineers will tell one that this is the case; even the most hard-headed will confess to a feeling of exhilaration in such surroundings, where man has had no impact, and even his presence on the peaks is no more than a speck of dust in the aeons of time taken to form the Cairngorms.

CHAPTER 9

Pleasure and Profit

Any visitor to the Spey Valley today may well be forgiven for thinking that the scenic delights of the area have always been there and that little has changed except for the growth of the original small settlements into large facilities for the tourist industry. In fact, over the last three centuries or so, massive and often drastic changes have taken place, all the result of Man's need for timber from the forests, new ground to plough, rivers to harness, and pleasure to be derived from the abundance of wild life, particularly its destruction.

After the Ice Age, which covered most of Britain, the massive slow-moving ice-sheets carved out the Cairngorms and prepared the way for the development of a variety of soil types which, at a later time, were to support a wide range of vegetation. By the time the first humans arrived, around 3000BC, the whole area was covered with dense forest which had to be cleared. The first human remains in the Spey Valley are of farming people who settled near Grantown. They were followed by others who started a process which has continued for some 4000 years. Fortunately for us today, a more enlightened attitude to land use prevails and we can enjoy what remains.

One of the major and continuing assets of the Highlands is the forests. In the past this largely comprised the Old Caledonian Forest, an extensive tract of woodland and scrub which, when man first entered Scotland, covered over half the Scottish mainland area below 3000 feet. In time the woods, a valuable source of fuel, building material and, later, charcoal, were depleted and only in the last century or so have attempts been made to replace the original land cover; but we have to accept that these attempts were made on a purely commercial basis and not with a view to restoring the countryside.

That the Old Caledonian Forest was of significant economic importance to the Highland region is clear from many documentary references to the uses to which wood was put: from firewood to shipbuilding. There was also the burning of

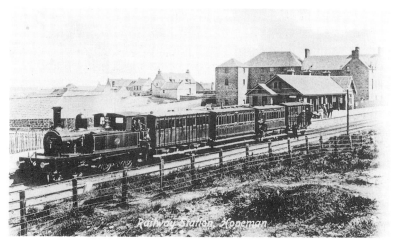

Hopeman station (Highland Railway) in Highland Railway days.
(Photograph: Lens of Sutton)

forest-covered area to extend land for cultivation. This, however, was carried out to such an extent that it was realised by the old Scots Parliament that a serious problem could arise which would have serious consequences for the future, if not in the lifetime of the contemporary politicians, then at least in that of a future generation. So legislation was introduced by the middle of the fifteenth century to regulate the destruction of forests, though, in reality, it had little effect.

Many woodlands were burnt to the ground to remove the natural cover of wolves as well as of human predators: criminals and outlaws for whom forests provided the perfect refuge. Later, iron foundries were established which further depleted the forests. By the end of the eighteenth century much of the original land cover as represented by the Old Caledonian Forest had disappeared, particularly in the Cairngorms and in the valley of the Spey. Perhaps the last major act of destruction was the clearance of tree cover to provide sheep runs on a vast scale which prevented natural regeneration.

Although the pastures thus produced were fertile to begin with, they degenerated rapidly as the result of the natural cycle of chemical and organic activity associated with forest cover being broken. Subsequent loss by leaching became more pronounced, there being no forest litter to retain a proportion of the rainfall at the surface. Downhill wash produced peat-forming processes. Bracken, once broken and bruised and kept in check by the hooves of grazing cattle, ran rife, because sheep and deer are selective grazers and avoid the spreading bracken-infested areas. One problem was compounded by another to produce the present sad picture of land degeneration in the Highlands. All these processes, however, produced an interesting panorama of economic exploitation which has added an extra dimension to the human history of the Spey Valley.

When Edward Burt travelled in the Highlands in the 1720s, he was impressed by the number of uses for timber, as a replacement for iron which was then in short supply: 'Almost all their implements for husbandry, which in other countries are made from iron, or partly of that metal, are in some parts of the Highlands made entirely of wood; such as the spade, plough-share, harrow, harness and bolts; and even locks for doors are made of wood'. Other uses included timber for house-building, furnishings, carts and other vehicles, boats, domestic utensils, basketwork, and ropes with tree bark, particularly oak, being used for tanning and dyeing.

But the overall use of tree produce was not particularly extravagant and the forests were well able to recover from the demands made on them. A certain amount of economy in the use of timber was also practised, as seen in the old custom of removing the main roof timbers of a house if the occupant decided to move to another part of the district. Roof timbers were in fact considered the property of the tenant and an asset over which the landowner had no control. It was this that led to these timbers being burnt during the period of the Highland Clearances, to prevent the evicted occupants from erecting a house elsewhere. Deprived of this important asset, the evicted were made truly homeless.

By the closing years of the seventeenth century however, the way timber was looked at had changed from a purely domestic and incidental use to a more commercial approach which introduced the new technique of forest management. Wood, particularly Scots pine, became a main attraction, along with the oak, the bark of which provided the main agent of the British tanning industry until the late nineteenth century. It was inevitable that commercial interests of a speculative nature would appear on the Highland forest scene. The York Buildings Company almost transformed the Spey Valley from an area of local importance to one of economic significance for the gross national product of Britain.

There were historical reasons for the introduction of this Company to the Highlands. In the seventeenth century feuds between clans and their septs, and civil wars involving Scottish military forces, reached their peak. Deeside, on the eastern side of the Cairngorms, was an area of frequent battles and skirmishes. Add to that the fact that the folk in the area of the Cairngorms were partly Catholic and pro-Jacobite, and the stage was set for change of a painful nature. In the year 1688, the Whig, General MacKay, burned no less than twelve miles of very fertile Highland country, involving the destruction of up to 1400 houses in upper Deeside.

The Jacobite Rising of 1715 was an event full of significance for the future of the Highlands and was to let in outside factors and influences which were able to take root and wrench the Highlands into contact with the social and economic world beyond. It was followed by another Jacobite Rising three decades later the failure of which marked the end of the old order: the clan chiefs who survived, instead of measuring wealth in terms of the number and loyalty of their armed followers, turned into landowners concerned with the potential of their land and timber for profitable exploitation.

Those chiefs who had not become involved with the Jacobites in 1715 were able to sit back and apply themselves to profit. But for those who had nailed their colours to the Jacobite mast, it was a different story. Their estates and titles became forfeit and attainted and their former lands came up for grabs to open up the way for outright exploitation. Thus, the York Buildings Company came on the Highland scene.

The Company was established in 1691 by an Act of Parliament which enabled the Company to raise the Thames water in York Buildings in London and supply customers in St James's and Piccadilly from its waterworks in the grounds of York House. The Company ended its long life in 1818 with the waterworks as its only asset, and that was worth a mere and literal peppercorn. But the years between 1691 and 1818 were to provide the Company and its directors with many opportunities for speculation and profit.

The improbable move from supplying water to London's great aristocratic houses to an involvement in agricultural and industrial operations in Scotland came about after the 1715 Rising. As soon as the Rising had been reduced to simmering point, with an effective lid placed on the efforts but not the aspirations of the Jacobites, a number of Highland estates were forfeited under the Acts of Attainder and were put up for sale. An Act of Parliament of 1719 empowered the purchasers of forfeited lands to grant annuities on the value of the estates, and to do this a coporate body was needed. By a coincidence, the York Buildings Company was offered for sale at the same time. A far-sighted London solicitor saw the possibility of using the Company as a means of amassing great profit and the Company was engineered into entering the Highland scene as a landowner; its presence was at times notorious and unorthodox. It also brought to the Highlands one Aaron Hill. He was a friend of the poets Savage and Thomson, and was himself a dramatist and poet, traveller, manager of Drury Lane Theatre, a dabbler in political economy and an enterprising projector of schemes for profit.

The first whiff of speculation for the Company arrived in the autumn of 1719 when the Government's Commissioners of Enquiry were ready to begin selling the estates of those members of the Scottish aristocracy and landowning class who had made the mistake of supporting the Jacobite cause. These lands were bought by representatives of the York Buildings Company, including the small estate of Rob Roy Macgregor at Inversnaid. The second whiff came in the person of Aaron Hill. He had behind him an impressive record of both success and failure; for instance, in the last year of Queen Anne's reign he had set up a Beech Oil Company, for making olive oil from the fruit of the beech tree, the advantages of which he promoted in poetic verse:

> *France shall no more her courted vineyards boast,*
> *But look with envy on our northern coast,*
> *Which now enriched with matchless oil and corn,*
> *Unequalled vintages shall soon adorn.*

Burghead station (Highland Railway) in Highland Railway days looking towards Hopeman. *(Photograph: Lens of Sutton)*

Hill also became deeply involved in a plan to settle a new plantation in South Carolina, the money for which he tried to raise by setting up a lottery; this, however, was declared to be illegal. But Hill was not without resource: if South Carolina was to prove a difficult venture, would not Scotland's woodlands provide a better scene for speculation? In 1726 he visited the great pinewoods of Abernethy, on Speyside, which belonged to the Laird of Grant. These had been reported on for the Commissioners for the Navy in 1704 as 'the likeliest to serve her Majesty and Government' in terms of ship timber. Aaron Hill thought so too. On his return to London he persuaded the directors of the York Buildings Company to purchase the timber as it stood. The idea appealed to the Company's principals and in January 1728 they bought 60,000 trees of the best and finest woods on the Grant estate, at a price of £7000. The wood was to be cut over a period of fifteen years.

The Company also took a lease for the same period of the Main and Meadow of Coulnakyle, in the neighbourhood of the woods. Hill's report to the Company was that the trees were fit to make main masts for the Navy's ships. However, when a specimen cargo was cut and sent to London it was discovered that the trees were unfit for this purpose, though fit for secondary uses. Cutting operations began in earnest and on a large scale, with houses being built for the work-force and mills and machinery erected. Many of the workmen were not paid in cash, but in promissory notes issued by William Stephens, an ex-Member of Parliament and ex-Governor of the State of Georgia, who became supervisor of the Company's operation on Speyside. Such was the esteem in which the Company was held, and such its credit and influence, that for a number of years these notes of hand circulated in the district and were acceptable as currency.

Aaron Hill put in an appearance at Abernethy to survey the practical outcome of his schemes. He was received with great honours. The Duchess of Gordon extended her hospitality to him; the local gentry all pressed to make his acquaintance and the Magistrates of both Inverness and Aberdeen presented him with the freedom of their burghs and entertained him with much respect. So carried away was he with his reception that he burst into a flowering of verse under the shadow of Cairngorm, amongst which was an address to his wife from 'the Golden Groves of Abernethy'. But good public relations, as engineered by Hill, were no compensation for the real engineering problems which the Company was experiencing with its timber operations.

Captain Edward Burt, who wrote when the operations were in full swing, doubted whether the Company would ever recover the costs of felling and removing trees from the area '. . . over rock, bogs, precipices, and conveyance by rocky rivers, except such as are near the sea coast, and hardly those, as I believe the York Buildings Company will find in the conclusion'. This was an intelligent prediction, for in the course of four years the charge on the timber trade had exceeded its returns by nearly £28,000.

Another observer was the Reverend John Grant, the parish minister, who wrote: '. . . the most profuse and profligate set that were ever heard of in this corner . . . This was said to be a stock-jobbing business. Their extravagancies of every kind ruined themselves and corrupted others. Their beginning was great indeed, with 120 working horses, waggons, elegant temporary wooden houses, saw-mills, iron-mills, and every kind of implement and apparatus of the best and most expensive sorts. They used to display their vanity by bonfires, tar barrels, and opening of hogsheads of brandy to the country people, by which five of them died in one night. They had a commisary for provisions and forage at a handsome salary, and in the end went off in debt to the proprietors and the country. But yet their coming to the country was beneficial in many respects, for besides the knowledge and skill which was acquired from them, they made many useful and lasting improvements. They made roads through the woods. They erected proper saw-mills. They invented the construction of the raft as it is at present, and cut a passage through a rock in Spey, without which floating to any extent could never be attempted'.

This minister, however much he expressed disapproval of the Company's influence on his flock, was not behind the door when it came to making the proverbial fast buck. When the workmen of the Company were paid in gold, they went to the Reverend Grant for change, which he provided at the rate of twenty shillings to the guinea.

The Napoleonic Wars created a big demand for the Abernethy timber. In 1797 'the rents of Rothiemurchus were small, not more than £800, but the timber was beginning to be marketable; three or four thousand a year could easily have been cut out of that forest and hardly have been missed'.

To diversify its operations, the Company set up iron furnaces in the neighbourhood where 'Glengarry' and 'Strathdown' iron pigs were produced, with another four furnaces set up to make bar iron. For these furnaces great quantities of timber were cut down in the Abernethy area. The amount of charcoal produced exceeded the requirements of the iron-making operations and large shipments of the material were sent to England and Holland. But the iron venture was no more profitable than the timber operation and large debts began to accrue against this side of the Company's interests.

On the Company's other business fronts, too, problems appeared daily and began to pile up into a huge legal mess which took until 1818 to sort out, when the Company's only asset was the original waterworks in London. Even that was being challenged by the New Chelsea Water Works, in the favour of which the York Buildings Company gave an undertaking not to engage to supply water, as a public water company, for a period of 2000 years, and demised the fee simple of their property, from September 1818, at a yearly rental of a peppercorn.

Thus some 150 years of operation by the Company were reduced to nothing by inexpertise. Even though the conduct of the Company's business showed much ingenuity, most of its schemes were wanting in honesty. It became over-burdened with capital speculations and failed to operate its various trading ventures with a view to profit. Decades of litigation cost a fortune; the legal battles which took place in Edinburgh's Court of Session are said to have cost the Company £3000 a year. Indeed, many of the decisions in these litigations have now become leading cases and it is said that contemporary questions in every department of company law have at one time been settled at the expense of the York Buildings Company. If Speyside, and Scotland as a whole, did not reap much lasting benefit from the Company's sojourn there, Scots lawyers gained a living from it.

Before the Company came along, however, the owners of the woodlands in the Spey Valley had been accustomed to float their timber down river; the logs were either single or in lots, loosely tied together and attended by men working from a 'currach' or coracle, a small basket of wickerwork covered on the outside with an animal skin. The actual rafting of timber had not been thought of until Aaron Hill arrived on the scene and introduced the method without delay. Large trees, with deals and boards, were bound together. On the top were placed the floaters who, armed with oars, conducted the rafts down the Spey to Garmouth. The local people soon learned to take advantage of this new means of transport and floated down their own rafts with their produce of butter, cheese, skins, bark and lime. Indeed, rafting on Highland rivers became something of a boon to new industries in the region and it was not until after Hill's introduction of rafting on the Spey that other Highland rivers carried on their waters massive quantities of cut timber to sawmillers and charcoal burners.

But before rafting could become commonplace, the river had to be tamed enough to take the rafts, and the rafters, or

Red Grouse. *(Photograph: David Gowans)*

floaters, retrained from sailing their small light currachs to navigating large masses of timbers through the waters of the Spey.

The currach was widely used in the Spey Valley as a means of transport. It was a flat-bottomed, slightly oval and almost tub-like affair, constructed with a frame of wickerwork over which was fitted the skin of a horse, cow or deer. The craft was fitted with a seat and equipped with a wooden paddle which looked something like a garden spade. The currach could be carried on a man's back, often for miles, to get to the waters of a Spey tributary. One man achieved some degree of fame for his stamina. Known as Alastair Mor na Curach, Alastair of the Coracle, he was a member of a group of families with a long association with timber-floating to Speymouth. The currach men were thus on the scene when the York Buildings Company arrived, and it was they, more than likely, who provided the incentive to Aaron Hill to form a scheme to exploit the Abernethy Woods. A description of these currach men dates from 1859: 'Two families of Grant, named Mor and Odhar, who lived at Tulchan, on the Spey, were the first who ventured on this perilous voyage. The first raft consisted of eight trees, fastened together by a hair rope. One or two men went into the currach to guide the raft, others from the shore, with ropes fastened to the tail end of the raft, acted as a rudder. On the second trip a dozen trees were brought down. The currach was always carried back from the mouth of the Spey on the back of a stalwart Highlander, who had obtained the name of Alastair Mor na Curach. This worthy occupied the farm of Dalcroy, on the Spey, and lived to the age of 106 years'.

It is thought that the Spey currach now preserved in Elgin Museum is the last of its kind in Scotland, and is the one used by Alastair Mor during the period of the timber-floating activities of the York Buildings Company.

Some of the first documentary mentions of the currach being used on the River Spey date back to the late fifteenth century, when the craft was used in connection with catching salmon with nets, and presumably used to take the men out to the nets to remove the fish. The currach men seem to have been employees of the local estate rather than fishers on their own account.

When the York Buildings Company bought its trees from the Laird of Grant in 1728, it also purchased the use of the existing sawmills of the River Nethy. In the early days of its operations, the Company had some 18 currachs employed in floating small rafts of sawn deals. Progress was slow, however, until Aaron Hill suggested that larger quantities of timber could be floated on rafts with advantage to the Company's profits.

Hill evolved a method of constructing a large raft 'conducted by two men, one at each end, who have each a seat and an oar, with which they help the raft in the proper direction'. Each of these larger rafts could carry up to £20-worth of timber at an average cost per raft per journey of £1 10s. The Spey had, however, to be made navigable by the removal of large rocks in the river. This was done by a method produced by Hill's fertile brain. When the water in the river was low, men made 'large fires on the rocks when the stream was low, and then throwing water on the heated surface. The stone was thus calcined or fractured and rendered easy of removal'.

The timber activities started by the Company in Abernethy continued for many decades, there being a constant demand for wood for many purposes, but particularly for the needs of war. Due to the shrinking supply in England, and the hazards of bringing timber from Scandinavia and far-off New Brunswick, it fell to the woods of Speyside to keep up with the demand. All this activity brought considerable trade to Upper Speyside and to the villages at the mouth of the river: Kingston and Garmouth. The activity had not escaped the attention of other landowners in Speyside and they, too, began to exploit their forests.

In 1794 it was reported that: 'The quantity of spars, deals, logs, masts and ship-timber, which they send to Garmouth or Speymouth yearly, is immense and every stage of the process of manufactory brings money to the country; generally once a year they send down Spey a loose float, as they call it, of about 12,000 pieces of timber of various kinds, whence they send it to England, or sell it round the coast. For some years they have sent great numbers of small masts or yards to England to the King's yards, and other places, and have built about twenty vessels of various burdens at Garmouth or Speymouth, all of Glenmore fir . . . The fir-woods of this country exceed all the natural fir-woods in Scotland put together, without comparison'.

Other documentary sources indicate that these 'loose floats', as distinct from the rafts, could number up to 20,000 logs and spars and were accompanied by up to eighty men who went along the riversides with long poles, pushing off the timber when it stuck. The men got 1s 6d a day, with free whisky rations. Rafts were still used, but only for sawn timber, and consisted of about fifty spars bound together on which deals and other sawn timber were laid. The rafters or floaters who saw these rafts safely down the Spey to Garmouth then returned home carrying on their shoulders the iron hooks and ropes used in making up the rafts.

The life of the floaters, while it had a certain romance, was hard and often dangerous. The life and work of the floaters is vividly described by Elizabeth Grant of Rothiemurchus in her book *Memoirs of a Highland Lady:* 'The logs prepared by the loppers had to be drawn by horses to the nearest running water, and left there in large quantities till the proper time for sending them down the streams. It was a busy scene all through the forest, so many rough little horses moving about in every direction, each dragging its load, attended by an active boy as guide and remover of obstructions . . . This driving lasted till sufficient timber was collected to render the opening of the sluices profitable . . . In order to have a run of water at command, the sources of the little rivers were managed artificially to suit floating purposes. Embankments were raised at the ends of the lakes in the far-away glens, at the point where the different burnies issued from them. Strong sluice-gates, always kept closed, prevented the escape of any but a small rill of water, so that when a rush was wanted the supply was sure.

'The night before a run, the man in charge of that particular sluice set off up the hill, and reaching the spot long before daylight opened the heavy gates; out rushed the torrent, travelling so quickly as to reach the deposit of timber in time for the meeting of the woodmen . . . The duty of some was to roll the logs into the water; this was effected with the help of levers . . . The next party shoved them off with long poles into the current, dashing in often up to the middle of the water when any case of obstruction occurred. They were then taken in charge by the most picturesque group of all, each supplied with a clip, a very long thin pole and flexible at one end, generally a young tall tree.

'A sharp hook was fixed to the bending point, and with this, skipping from rock to stump, over brooks and through briers, this agile band followed the log-laden current, ready to pounce on any stray lumbering victim that was in any manner checked in its progress. There was something graceful in the action of throwing forth the stout yet yielding clip, an exciting satisfaction as the sharp hook fixed the obstreperous log. The many light forms springing about the trees, along the banks that were sometimes high, and always rocky, the shouts, the laughter, the Gaelic exclamations, and above all, the roar of the water, made the whole scene one of the most inspiriting that either actors or spectators could be engaged in.

'The Spey floaters lived mostly down near Ballindalloch, a certain number of families by whom the calling had been followed for ages, to whom the wild river, all its holes and shoals and rocks and shiftings, were as well known as had its

Queen Victoria on Fyvie, with John Brown, by G. W. Wilson.
(Scottish National Portrait Gallery)

bed been dry. They came up in the season, at the first hint of a
spate, as a rise in the water was called. A large bothy was built
for them at the mouth of the Druie in a fashion that suited
themselves; a fire on a stone hearth in the middle of the floor,
a hole in the very centre of the roof just over it where some of
the smoke got out, heather spread on the ground, no window,
and there, after their hard day's work, they lay down for the
night, in their wet clothes – for they had been perhaps hours in
the river – each man's feet to the fire, each man's plaid round
his chest, a circle of wearied bodies half stupefied by whisky,

enveloped in a cloud of steam and smoke, and sleeping soundly till morning.'

Rafting on the Spey was not without its hazards. Often, rafts would be swept out to sea at the mouth of the river, across the bar of sand and shingle and its crew never seen again, particularly if the incident occurred in the dense sea mists which frequently occur along the coast of the Moray Firth. Men were also lost in accidents during felling operations and, in particular, by being crushed by heavy logs in the rivers.

Apart from timber-felling for shipbuilding and other purposes, the valuable iron deposits in the Tomintoul district made deep inroads into the Abernethy woods. The York Buildings Company erected smelting works near Nethy Bridge and the wood from the adjacent forests was made into charcoal. Innumerable horses were used to carry the basic iron ore in panniers over the hills for the distance of fifteen miles which separated the mines from Nethy Bridge. The ore contained a certain percentage of manganese, which was separated and taken, again by hill ponies, to Garmouth for shipment to the south. This enterprise, like the timber operation, failed to produce a profit and eventually only traces of the iron works remained in the neighbourhood of Abernethy.

The proximity of so much timber to the mouth of the Spey made it almost inevitable that shipbuilding would become established as an industry, and it fell to the small coastal settlement of Kingston to fill the role. Originally known as the Port of Garmouth, with the larger and much older village lying less than a mile from it to the east, it received its English name at the end of the eighteenth century.

Its economic importance began when two timber merchants from Kingston-on-Hull set up business in the village; they were known as raff merchants who specialised in importing timber in sawn deals. Their keen Yorkshire minds saw an obvious advantage in exporting their timber in the form of ships, using some of these to carry timber to the markets in the south. Though no trace remains of the former shipyard, it was an extremely busy place in its day, with the ships being launched into the sea and then warped inside the mouth of the Spey for outfitting and completion.

It was 1786 when these two men from Yorkshire, Osbourne and Dodsworth, set up their shipyard. During the first decade about 25 vessels were built and then a further 30 until the yard closed in 1815, the year of Waterloo. That historic event rang down the curtain on the immensely costly and ruinous Napoleonic Wars and introduced a period of financial exhaustion and a severe slump in trade. The closure then, as nowadays, threw many men out of work and Kingston became a backwater.

The largest ship built in the yard was the *Lady Madeline Sinclair*, named after the daughter of the fourth Duke of Gordon. The vessel was bought by the East India Company and was used for the India and China trades.

The closure of the yard caused a number of shipwrights to look to their future and not a few of them decided to emigrate to the Miramichi district of New Brunswick to take up work with a William Davidson from Inverness, who was building ships to carry salmon produce to the Mediterranean and other ports in Europe. The connection between Kingston and Miramichi was further strengthened by a quirk of fate.

On a voyage from New Brunswick to Sunderland, with a cargo of timber, the brig *Adventurer* was totally wrecked on the treacherous sand and shingle bar at the mouth of the Spey while running for shelter in a storm. The crew were saved by the efforts of a young man, Alexander Geddie, whose father, a shipwright, was himself on the point of emigrating to New Brunswick. Geddie *père* decided to gamble on buying the wreck of the *Adventurer*, which he refloated by means of herring barrels tied to the stricken ship. Making use of the facilities in the deserted shipyard at Kingston, he restored the ship to seaworthiness and sold her at a handsome profit, which he used to build a new shipyard that was to last for three-quarters of a century.

Where the canny Yorkshiremen had pulled out in the face of a national depression in the industry, the local man set his face against the odds and succeeded. Some 350 ships were to be built at the Kingston yard, exclusive of fishing craft. After the Geddie yard closed down the family emigrated to Natal. Many years later an old chest was discovered in which there were many constructional details of the ships built at Kingston. The find was valuable in that in those days many ships were constructed by rule of thumb and the shipwrights relied little on draughtsmanship. These documents now rest in the Science Museum, South Kensington, London, and fill a gap in the shipbuilding records of the time.

Also closely associated with the Geddies in shipbuilding at Kingston were the Kinloch family, who thrived with the Geddies in an age when most of the world trade was moving away from the small ports or open beaches used by comparatively small ships. Not only did Strathspey provide timber, but the countryside was not disturbed by the internal strife or wars which periodically put their Continental rivals out of business. These were the days when Britain truly ruled the waves and any ship flying the red duster received preferential treatment in most foreign ports. The Kinlochs celebrated this prosperity by naming one of their ships *Britannia*.

In all, the Kinlochs built over fifty ships and most of these were 99-ton schooners. Two vessels a year were launched and in their best twelve months 1400 tons of new shipping took to the open sea. Many of the ships were built for local owners and engaged in world trade. The largest vessel was the 800-ton barque *Lord MacDuff*. Owned by Captain MacDonald of Garmouth and engaged in the China trade, she was referred to as the 'Mighty MacDuff' in Moray Firth waters.

In the early 1880s the fortunes of Speymouth began to change: steam was replacing sail and the River Clyde took the lead by building in steel. Worse still, the inland forests of Speyside were becoming exhausted and timber had to be brought in from the Baltic and North America. Finally, the River Spey changed its course, leaving Garmouth very definitely an inland port and Kingston the quiet settlement it is today.

Some of the history, and indeed mystery, of the sea attaches to Kingston. One ship built there was destined to go on one of the expeditions in search of Sir John Franklin in the Arctic. Another, the *Chieftain* was to make her name as a China tea-clipper and was considered to have had a sporting chance of winning the 1858 homeward race from Hong Kong with the first cargo of that season's tea. While she did not win that race, she did reach London in less than the magic 100 days.

One Kingston-built ship was the subject of a sea mystery. She was the *Satellite*, a barquentine of 300 tons built by the Geddie yard in 1867. She sailed for Valparaiso in 1869 and then was not heard of for some months. At first it was thought she had gone down in a storm with all hands, until she was seen in a South American port and then in Rio de Janeiro. An attempt was made to catch up with her, but she disappeared again, to be traced, finally, to Baltimore, where the captain was arrested for piracy. Unfortunately there was a lack of documentary evidence and the necessary witnesses, and the master escaped scot free. In those days it was possible for a ship's master to have full control of the chartering of his owner's vessel, and to handle cash payments for freights carried; thus, many a sea captain was able to retire early on the proceeds of illegal transactions.

Today, when the visitor to Speyside strolls among the woods of Abernethy and Glenmore, or takes a leisurely walk along the banks of the Spey, the Druie or the Nethy, history is a companion whose presence can only enhance his interest in the area and perhaps cause him to reflect on the natural wealth of Speyside which once provided employment, profit, loss and a vibrant and colourful past.

From the exploitation of the woodland resources of the Spey Valley in the eighteenth century to the exploitation of its scenic resources in the mid-nineteenth and twentieth centuries is but a step in the same direction. The preservation of a vulnerable environment is causing concern to conservationists, just as others are worried about the social implications of subjecting the area to intensive economic development as the need increases for 'wilderness areas' for the benefit of those whose normal environments fail to offer relaxation and leisure pursuits.

Mountain soils are often at great risk from the increased numbers tramping over them, as are the plant communities which rely on them for their continuity. Damage is most apparent on the soils and vegetation near ski-lifts. Added to that is the scarring of areas for tourist development, the pollution of certain lochs and streams and the thoughtless scattering of non-biodegradable litter than cannot be broken down by normal weathering processes. One can understand why there is concern. Fortunately this concern is being taken on board by some of those very tourists who visit the Cairngorms and learn something of the delicate balances which exist in the area. Many become active conservationists and treat delicate and sensitive areas with respect.

When the skiing industry started in the 1960s, pistes were opened up in the Cairngorms. Much bulldozing took place, destroying Arctic-Alpine vegetation above the timber line. Then skiing was allowed during periods of thin snow when vegetation was most vulnerable to damage. As soon as the natural vegetation was crushed, bare soil was exposed and soil erosion set in. Remedial action was taken by the construction of snow fences to catch snow on the ski runs. Pylons and concrete for new ski lifts were flown in by helicopter to avoid damaging the ground. Attempts were also made to restore by reseeding damaged vegetation at the end of each skiing season. The concern of the ski operators was of course welcome as an indication of an appreciation of the balance that had to be maintained between the needs of leisure and pleasure and those of the environment.

New problems are now being discovered. Marked changes have been observed in the natural Alpine flora near ski-lifts. On and near the ski grounds the breeding success of ptarmigan and red grouse has suffered due to the lack of insect life in the reseeded damaged ground. The birds' breeding is also suffering from predation by crows, whose population is thriving on the scraps of sandwiches and other food left by tourists. By 1981 no ptarmigans were breeding on the more heavily developed parts of the Coire Cas ski grounds at Cairngorm.

In 1981 a public inquiry was held to consider the pros and cons of the ski development proposed for Lurcher's Gulley. The outcome was that the Secretary of State for Scotland recognised the outstanding scientific and recreational value of this area, and rejected the planning application. But the Secretary added that had the development not been so ambitious, it might have been more acceptable. The inquiry led to published guidelines for ski developers, identifying four main areas for ski development, and giving advice on lessening damage to the environment. Now development creeps ahead on the coat-tails of small-scale plans.

It might be said that the Spey Valley tourist industry began when the old Highland estates were broken up and converted into sporting areas. This was a development which led to depopulation and inferior forms of land use. Of course, then it was only the rich who could afford either to buy or rent land for their enjoyment and it was to these that the landowners looked to supplement their incomes.

One of the first, if not the first, to recognise the possibilities of Highland estates for sport with gun and rod was the indomitable Colonel Thomas Thornton, an eccentric Yorkshire squire who pioneered the English sporting invasion of the Highlands. In 1804 he wrote *Sporting Tour in the Northern Part of England and Great Part of the Highlands of Scotland*, having visited the Highlands some twenty years previously.

Around 1783 he was in the Badenoch area on a reconnoitring visit, 'living during the time he was there in tents'. This visit was in the nature of a preparation for his big tour which was conducted in 1786 in the grand style. Some idea of the extent of his baggage may be got from the fact that he hired a cutter, the *Falcon*, to take his creature comforts from Hull to Fochabers; so extensive were his requirements that it needed forty-nine carts to take them all from Fochabers to Badenoch, while four more horses were employed to transport on a sledge two large boats for his own use on the lochs. To the natives of Strathspey, the colonel's cavalcade must have seemed ominous as the invading army wound its slow way among the hills.

He first resided at Raitts, two miles north of Kingussie, in rented accommodation, from which base he made many excursions into the immediate areas. He was one of the first contributors to depopulation. He insisted that he be given full possession of Linwilg, which led to the removal of the farming folk living there.

The colonel recorded some of his 'bags'. In Dulnain at Carrbridge: '. . . the game on these moors is innumerable. In a mile long, and not one half broad, I saw at least 1000 brace of birds [red grouse]'. He recorded a fantastic gamebag of 561 birds and mammals of fifteen species, and 1126 fish.

The colonel's exploits and the size of his gamebags drew Strathspey to the notice of others and they followed him into

Badenoch. Invertromie was reported to be abounding, 'with hill and dale and well stocked with game, and allowed by most people to be an excellent quarter for a sportsman', the latter being Colonel Gordon, styled as Glentromie, who once 'brought his brood of five sons up to Glentromie in a boat set on wheels which, after performing coach on the roads, was used for loch fishing in the hills'.

The takeover of land in the Spey Valley continued with the displacement of the local population by those who could afford to buy or lease estates. Writing in 1848, one Robert Somers was critical of the landlords and the large tenant farmers he met, describing the latter as having been 'raised to a position of wealth and indolence over the necks of the people'. He wrote that their prosperity had been a direct cause of pauperism and that they grudged paying even a trifling contribution to the poor rate. He describes his visit to Badenoch: '. . . a great proportion of the farms are occupied by gentlemen who were at one time connected with the army. A stranger is amazed at the majors, and captains, and lieutenants, with whom he finds a peaceable country so thickly planted; and as they are all Macphersons or Mackintoshes, he is apt to get completely bewildered in attempting to preserve their respective identities. These gentlemen are officers who received their commissions from the Duchess of Gordon and who, on returning home from the wars, founded upon their services in the field a claim to a comfortable agricultural settlement. Their demand was allowed, but these military farmers, generally speaking, have not been successful . . . To make room for these gentlemen of the army, the small farmers were pushed to the wall. While the village of Kingussie was in a growing state, it offered asylum to the people thus cleared from the land; and when its population began to run over, a smaller village, called Newtonmore, received its refuse. In these two villages, and in a few small crofts scattered over the barren spots of the parish, have been deposited the dregs of wretchedness, which here, as elsewhere, have been produced by extensive clearances'.

The real opening up of the Highlands as a tourist attraction came with Sir Walter Scott's writings; his letters, narrative poems and novels described an attractive alternative to the Grand Tour of Europe which, until the 1830s, had been considered essential for those who wished to add a final polish to their education. Another shot in the arm was given by the visits of Queen Victoria and her purchase of estates in the Deeside Highlands. Grouse shooting had begun to be fashionable by the 1820s; by 1850 the letting of grouse moors was common practice.

The end of the beginning came when the steam train puffed its way north to create centres of accommodation such as Boat of Garten and Aviemore in the 1860s. Indeed, it was the advent of the old Highland Railway which created the basis of the village of Aviemore as it is now known. The original settlement there provided no fewer than 140 employees for much-needed work on the railway.

Although the Highlands caught the tail-end of the railway fever which swept through Britain in the early days of the commercial iron road, the fever was no less intense and produced many rival schemes. Part of the reason for the opening of the Inverness-Perth rail route was the need to transport timber from the Strathspey woodlands. By the mid-nineteenth century neither the old method of floating logs down the Spey, nor the road transport available, was entirely suitable for large quantities. So it was not surprising that two prominent landowners, the Earl of Seafield and Thomas Bruce, became leading promoters of the Inverness and Perth Junction Railway, which was to find itself constantly in conflict with the Great North of Scotland Railway which offered to take passengers from Inverness to the south via Aberdeen, a long and tedious journey. In 1860 the directors of the Inverness and Perth Junction Railway decided to revive an unsuccessful rail scheme of 1845, with the engineer in both schemes being Joseph Mitchell, a brilliant engineer with a long record to his credit of road, bridge and harbour schemes in the Highlands.

The plan as redrawn in 1860 had the route passing through Boat of Garten and Grantown, instead of Carrbridge. One reason for this was that both Seafield and Bruce wanted the railway to pass close to their estates. Indeed, had there not been this provision to recruit their support, the railway would not have been built. The route was constructed at a cost of £900,000 and the Aviemore/Boat of Garten/Forres section of the line was opened in August 1863. The direct line from

Aviemore to Inverness was opened in November 1898 following fierce disputes between the Highland Railway Company and the Great North of Scotland Railway. While the new routes carried a certain amount of freight in the form of timber and livestock, passenger traffic was slow to grow and along with it the tourist trade. But the railway did make it possible for large numbers of people to get north into areas which previously had been as remote to them as were parts of Central Africa.

At first the summer visitors were from the wealthier classes who came on shooting and fishing safaris, sometimes in the special carriages they hired for their large parties. Afterwards, tourism became more broadly based, and by the 1900s the railway was catering for a wide range of people on their excursions to Inverness and farther north. Summer traffic tended to peak just before the start of the grouse season on 12 August. Hitherto isolated communities in the Spey Valley began to cater for the incoming visitors, and small inns, such as that at Boat of Garten with only one public room, mushroomed into full-blown hotels.

In the Edwardian period, holiday homes for families from the south were built in Kingussie and Aviemore. It was not until 1914 that motor traffic began to make inroads on the railway and subsequent improvements to the Perth-Inverness A9 road further reduced the numbers of holidaymakers coming into the area by train. Changes in the type of tourist were reflected in the growth of boarding-house facilities, with no fewer than twenty having been built in Boat of Garten alone by 1939.

The setting up of the Aviemore complex gave the railway a welcome boost: whereas before 1965 Aviemore, for example, was little more than a junction, it is now an important source of traffic in both summer and winter. At the same time, through passenger traffic on the Perth-Inverness line has increased, and the place now buzzes with tourist activity from the estimated million and more people who visit the area each year.

The Spey Valley, one of the fresh-air lungs of Europe, is still a focus of national attention, with more plans for further development to provide the widest range possible of tourist facilities.

And so history repeats itself in Strathspey. Private enterprise and financial speculation placed the area on the map when the York Building Company took up the challenge of exploitation and created far-reaching changes that have continued for two and a half centuries. Today, pleasure and profit is still the name of the game.

CHAPTER 10

The Whisky Trail

What is whisky? There are many answers to that question, but none comes close to the truth. Chemists know what it contains, yet even with that knowledge they are unable to produce in the laboratory a liquid which compares with a product which is based on centuries of knowledge, expertise and not a little cunning.

The water, on its own, is not the secret, for there are a number of distilleries which make use of the same source of water; yet their respective products have different tastes. Even barley from the same source can be treated to yield a different end product. The peat used to dry malted barley differs from place to place in the aroma it gives off when burned. Then comes the air of the Highland hills and glens, to enter into the process in some inexplicable manner. Last, but certainly not least, the distiller's expertise has to be taken into account. His art and craft represents a continuous element in the distilling process. Whisky, then, is a magical alchemical mix of a number of indefinable elements all of which go to make up a product which is uniquely associated with Scotland in general but, in particular, Speyside. Whisky can also be said to be derived from the four elements: air, earth, fire and water.

In the lower reaches of the Spey Valley there are more whisky distilleries to the square mile than in any other part of Scotland. This fact has been of major importance for the socio-economic welfare of many small communities in the region. Their contribution to the national exchequer is far from being small. Indeed, it has been estimated that the value of Scotch whisky currently in bond represents a sum which exceeds the total gold reserves in Britain. Fort Knox in liquid form!

The origins of whisky are lost somewhere in the dark centuries of antiquity. The process of distillation, however, has been recorded as far back as the fourth century BC, when Aristotle observed that sea water could be made drinkable by distillation. Its advent in Scotland is quite obscure. It is

George Smith 1792-1871. *(Courtesy The Glenlivet Distillery)*

plausibly suggested that the ancients in the East (the word 'alcohol' is derived from Arabic *'alkuhl'*) having held for long that cereals and spirits were important ingredients for a long life, revealed their secrets to the passing Celts on their way through Europe to the western fringes of the Atlantic. The Celts, being naturally ingenious, combined the two into an elixir and called it *uisge beatha,* the water of life, from which the word whisky is derived.

The Celts settled in Ireland with their new-found discovery, whence, it is said, it was transmitted to Scotland. No doubt the monks in old monasteries had a hand in perfecting the techniques, for among the more important centres of distilling are, or were, Islay, Kintyre and Speyside, all sites of monastic communities in earlier times.

Eventually the liquid came to be recognised as both food and medicine: 'that malt spirit which commonly served both for victual and drink'. Conditions in Scotland are ideal for the production of whisky: fresh, pure mountain air, locally-grown barley, nurtured by a warm and kindly sun, pure burn water 'off granite through peat', and, lastly, the rich peat which gives off such a pungent aroma when burned.

The first mention of whisky in Scotland occurs in an entry in the Exchequer Rolls for the year 1494: 'To Friar John Cor, by order of the King, to make aquavitae, VIII bolls of malt'. Thereafter whisky is mentioned with increasing frequency. By 1597, however, its popularity created a problem: widespread distilling, by folk both highborn and low, was causing a famine in grain supplies for solid food. An Act of that year states: 'Forasmuch as it appears that victuals shall be scarce this present year, and understanding that there is a great quantity of malt consumed in all parts of this realm in the making of aqua-vitae, this is one great reason for the dearth within the same. It lays down, therefore, that only Earls, Lords, Barons and Gentlemen, for their own use, shall distil any'.

From that time, whisky appears consistently in official records and, just as consistently, is made the subject of repressive measures to restrict its appeal to the common folk. Even so, the making of whisky was a regular and commonplace activity in many crofting and farmhouse kitchens; at some stage a surplus of liquor was produced which was either bartered for goods or simply sold for cash. It was appearing on the market in sufficient quantities to cause the English Government in 1660 to impose a duty of 2d per gallon on any such liquor imported south of the Border.

In 1644 the Scots Parliament in Edinburgh passed an Act of Excise, which fixed a sum of 2s 8d Scots per pint for whisky and similar strong liquor. By 1657 the trade in 'strong drink' was sufficient for the Parliament to set up a system for regulating the growing industry, in the form of 'gaugers', officers who had the power to gauge or measure containers used in the distillation process. Later years were to see the imposition of taxes on the brewing of home spirit.

In many Highland parishes the golden liquid was being made in sufficient quantities to constitute a secondary employment, and it was freely available at all times. In the eighteenth century it was quite common to have a glass of whisky as part of one's breakfast. Whisky also attracted some attention as a special food and medicine. In 1736 it was reported: 'The ruddy complexion, nimbleness of these people is not owing to the water drinking but to the aqua-vitae, a malt spirit which is commonly used both as victual and drink'. That was also the year in which John Porteous, Captain of the Edinburgh City Guard, was lynched.

That incident had its origin in the Treaty of Union of 1707 between England and Scotland. In that year there was a malt tax in England but not in Scotland, a point of difference considered so important that the Articles of Union provided that malt should not be taxed in Scotland. A period of grace was allowed until 1713 when the Westminster Government decided to extend the English tax into Scotland. It was met with vigorous opposition and the slogan 'Free Malt'. But by 1725 the Government won the day and the tax was imposed.

It was an ill-considered move. Trouble blew up in the faces of authority and became known as the Malt Tax Riots. Active opposition mushroomed to the extent that the military had to be mobilised to quell riots all over Scotland. Even General Wade, busy enough on a road-surveying expedition in the Highlands, was diverted from his duties to make haste to Glasgow to impose law and order. Rioters attacked the houses of Scots Members of Parliament and reduced them to ruins. In Edinburgh the mob ran amok and poor Captain Porteous paid the price for being in the right place at the wrong time.

Despite the troubles the taxes created, the Government was determined to derive some revenue from whisky and gradually tightened its grip on the embryo industry. The reaction was inevitable: the appearance of the professional smuggler, particularly in the Highlands. Another ill-considered move was made in 1780 when heavy duties were imposed on wines. This led to a greatly stimulated demand for good whisky, and the manufacture of illicit whisky became an almost universal practice during the next twenty years. Smuggling blossomed to the point where the licensed distillers, finding their market eroded, fell to producing inferior liquor, which however failed to recover their former custom. Indeed the whisky thus produced was so rank that it rarely compared with the 'pure and wholesome' malt liquor which was smuggled down from the Highlands to lowland markets.

In desperate reaction, the Government introduced various Acts of Parliament to control the production of illicit whisky, all of which failed to do anything other than consolidate the position of the smuggler. Whisky became the most legislated subject in the United Kingdom.

A final attempt to resolve the situation was the Act of 1814 which required payment of the sum of £10 for a licence to distil and the prohibition of stills of under 500 gallons – meaning that all small home brewers and distillers in the Highlands found themselves on the wrong side of the law, with their main source of income threatened. It was particularly hard on the poorer folk whose only source of cash was distilling, to help to pay the rents. What the Government also failed to realise was that the produce of these small distilleries was of a very high quality which attracted a steady demand. Indeed some distillers became bynames for quality. One such was George Smith of Glenlivet, whose still was one of about 200 in operation in that area of Speyside which still boasts the largest number of distilleries in Scotland.

George Smith was born in 1792, the son of a Glenlivet farmer. He began his working life as a builder and architect but abandoned these activities when his father died, to take over the family farm at Upper Druimin. He concentrated on the small-scale distilling operation on the farm which, under his direction, became very profitable. His excellent 'Glenlivet' made its way south through the glens to appreciative samplers of the beverage, among whom was numbered no less a personage than Sir Walter Scott.

In the latter's narrative poem 'St Ronan's Well', Sir Bingo treats the Captain and Doctor to some Glenlivet, which causes the Captain to exclaim: 'By Cot, it is the only liquor for a gentleman to drink in the morning, if he can have the good fortune to come by it, you see'. This accolade, it should be noted, was accorded to a whisky which was at that time regarded by the Government as being illegal.

Another tribute to 'Glenlivet' was offered by James Hogg, the Ettrick Shepherd: 'Give me the real Glenlivet, and I well believe I could mak' drinking toddy oot o' sea-water. The Human mind never tires o' Glenlivet, ony mair than o' caller air. If a body could just find oot the exact proportion and quantity that ought to be drunk every day, and keep to that, I verily trow that he might leeve for ever, without dying at a', and the doctors and kirkyards would go oot o' fashion'.

While these eulogies raised the 'Glenlivet' to legendary status, they were nothing compared with the final accolade, which was conferred on the liquid by none other than King George IV who paid a memorable visit to Edinburgh in the autumn of 1822, having been persuaded to do so by Sir Walter Scott. The King, having been introduced to Glenlivet, took to it so much that it remained his favourite tipple for the rest of his life, illegal though it was. The story is told that during the Edinburgh visit, supplies of Glenlivet ran out and the Chamberlain, Lord Conyngham, failed to find any, though he searched everywhere. But rescue was at hand – in the cellar of Sir John Grant – from Speyside, where else? A cask of Glenlivet was prepared and sent, along with fifty brace of prime ptarmigan, to Holyrood House, and was received with great relief. That generous gesture earned Sir John a judgeship in India. Seldom has an affinity to whisky produced such handsome results!

But to obtain 'Glenlivet', and the other superb products of Speyside pot stills, was not easy, either for the now-famous George Smith or for others. The presence of the gauger, or exciseman, always introduced an element of adventure, not to say danger, for the smuggler and his regular convoys of hardy Highland ponies with their precious cargoes strapped to their sides, stepping along the whisky trails in the lonely hills. A contemporary account describes these convoys ' . . . in bands of ten to twenty men, with as many horses, with two ankers of whisky on the back of each horse, wending their way, singing in joyous chorus, along the banks of the Avon'. On many occasions interception by excisemen led to fights, often to the death; the profession carried its occupational hazards to the limit. One successful exciseman, Malcolm Gillespie, on the day of his death in 1827, was able to point to forty-two wounds on various parts of his body, sustained in the course of twenty-eight years' unflinching service.

The year in which moonshine became daylight was 1823, when the Illicit Distillation (Scotland) Act came into being. The Act laid down stiff penalties for all offences connected with illicit distilling. Huge fines, with increased powers for excisemen, created problems for smugglers and distillers alike.

George Smith decided that if he could not operate illegally, then he would make whisky with the blessing of the Act. He therefore took out a licence for his bothy, rebuilt and remodelled his distillery, and made Glenlivet 'official'. But it was no easy transition. His fellow-smugglers regarded him as a traitor and gave him a rough time of it.

He had to carry around with him at all times a pair of hair-trigger pistols and never went on his travels alone. He received many threats of physical injury and the burning of his distillery to the ground. For some years he lived on a knife-edge but won through until a new kind of opposition appeared. Attracted by the realisation that the Glenlivet area produced excellent whisky, other distilling interests appeared on the scene to cash in on the reputation of the original 'Glenlivet'. In 1880, after a long legal tussle, a High Court Order was secured making Smith's whisky the only one entitled to the name 'The Glenlivet', without a hyphenated prefix indicating the name of a particular distillery.

The most southerly Speyside distillery is at Dalwhinnie. But most are concentrated in the northern reaches of the River Spey and its tributaries, to the north and east of Grantown on Spey – there are nearly fifty distilleries, each with its own unique flavour.

There are three principal varieties of whisky produced in Scotland today: malt, grain and blended. Malt whisky, usually Highland, is made entirely from a watery extract of malted barley, fermented by the addition of yeast and then twice-distilled in the characteristic onion-shaped pot stills, from which the flavoured alcohol is driven off by heat. The still has to be recharged after each distillation. Highland-made malt whisky differs from its Lowland counterpart in that the former has its malted barley dried in the kiln over a peat fire. It is the combustion fumes of the peat which endow the whisky with that subtle smokiness which, in discreet combination with other flavours, is the hallmark of a genuine Highland whisky. Malt whisky takes from ten to fifteen years in oak casks to mature properly.

Different malts take different periods to come to that stage of maturity at which the whisky reaches its peak in performing miracles on the taste buds. Many single malts (those which are

The Whisky Centre and Museum at Inverdruie.
(Photograph: Hamish Brown)

not blended with other malts) are put on the market at ten years of age. Others, however, tend to take longer to reach their peak of perfection. There are some malts on the market which are over twenty years old, although they are few and far between. However, certain malts of that age are available bottled from the cask by private organisations such as the Scotch Malt Whisky Society, or by independent bottlers.

In 1987 eight bottles of 60-year-old malt from the Macallan Distillery were sold for £5500 each at an auction which attracted postal bids from connoisseurs from around the world. It is not recorded whether the liquid was drunk or kept as an investment.

Most malt whisky production goes for blending. Blended whisky is a mixture of matured and grain whiskies, thus securing the lighter quality of the grain with the unmistakable flavour of the malts. The practice of blending pot-still and patent-still whiskies began about 1860 to cater largely for the 'home', or southern, markets. Blending is a skilled task: as many as thirty or more different single malts may be mixed with the almost neutral, or 'silent', grain spirit.

Grain whisky is made mostly from imported maize (American corn), but rye and oats can also be used. After mashing, with the addition of a little malted barley, it is fermented and then distilled in a Coffey or patent still, where the alcohol is driven off by steam. It is possible with this type of still to produce a spirit with a 95 per cent alcohol content in one continuous operation. This is the means by which the bulk of industrial alcohol is made; at one time a large proportion of the raw product went to London to be made into gin or methylated spirits.

There are many arguments as to whether this spirit made in a patent still is entitled to the name 'whisky'. Indeed it took a Royal Commission in 1909 to recognise the newcomer and give it equal status with the spirit produced in the more traditional manner. The commercial lobby was, however, more powerful than the opposition who represented the genuine liquid. Grain whisky is lighter and chemically purer than malt whisky, but has a much less distinctive flavour. It matures more quickly but does not improve in the cask to anything like the extent of malt whisky; it is also cheaper to make, which of course is a prime commercial attraction.

At the end of the day it is the palate of the individual which will dictate the choice. There are available many single malts which are sold in retail outlets and in hostelries which have weaned the drinkers of blends over to the malts. Indeed, their popularity has increased, and now many bars make a point of displaying a satisfying range of single malts.

Like all industries with an international market, whisky distilling is continually subject to financial considerations as seen in takeover bids and the case of the Glen Grant Distillery at Rothes: new stills were opened in 1978 at a cost of around £500,000 to increase production by about one million gallons a year. In 1970 several of the Spey distilleries amalgamated to form the Glenlivet Distillers Ltd; however, to ensure its survival the company had to sell out to Seagrams, the Canadian group, for £50 million, ending the Grant family connection which had stretched back over 144 years.

As part of the general promotion of malt whisky, several Speyside distilleries have combined their interests and set up the only Malt Whisky Trail in the world. The Trail begins at Strathisla in the town of Keith to the east of Speymouth Forest. Strathisla was established in 1786 and is fondly regarded as the oldest operating distillery in the Highlands. It takes its water from the Broomhill spring, which rises in the hill above the distillery. Its long history includes a destructive fire in 1876 which not only ruined part of the distillery but roasted 30 of the 66 cows in a nearby farm byre. In 1950 the distillery was bought by Chivas Brothers, the provision merchants of Aberdeen, after the distillery had gone through a rather 'interesting' period at the hands of a financier who was found guilty of tax evasion. 'Strathisla' has a wholesome aromatic taste and a pleasant fruity, pungent bouquet.

South of Keith lies Dufftown, the second stage of the Trail, and the Glenfiddich distillery. Built in 1886 by William Grant, who invested his entire capital of £775 in the venture, this is the only Speyside distillery to bottle its own whisky. It is said that Grant built the distillery in Dufftown after being told by an old priest of the existence of the Robbie Dubh spring, whose waters were both pure and inexhaustible. At first Grant worked on his own, then he brought in his three sons who had to carry on with their own education while working as stillmen, maltmen and tun-roon men. The story is told of a vist by a representative of the Inland Revenue. He found Latin and mathematical textbooks lying all over the place. On enquiry he was told that they belonged to the sons. Two of them became doctors and the third became the owner of Glendronach distillery. The distillery is still family-owned. It is reckoned that over 50,000 free drams are given away each year to visitors to its popular reception centre. 'Glenfiddich' has a good and satisfying touch on the palate: soft, delicate and with a hint of peat.

The third distillery is reached by the road south through Glen Rinnes, past the heights of Meikle Conval and Ben Rinnes: Tamnavulin. It takes its name from an old watermill nearby. The mill provided the power needed to card wool from the sheep which roamed round the foothills of the Cairngorms. The distillery was built in 1966. The old mill was converted into a visitor centre and the old mill wheel has been restored to its former glory. It is a modern complex and provides a sharp contrast to the older distilleries. The product is light and delicate with a pleasant smokey finish.

'The Glenlivet' distillery is the fourth stop on the trail. Although this is not George Smith's original distillery (he had two: at Drumin and Delnabo), the product has his original cachet. It was built in 1858 on a hillside where the Livet water flows to join the River Avon. A battle was fought in this area in 1594 between the Royal Army, under the command of the Earl of Huntly, and the Covenanting forces led by the Duke of Argyll. It was a bloody battle, at least on the Covenanting side, with their losses amounting to 500 compared with Huntly's losses of 14. The water for the distillery comes from springs rising in the Braes of Glenlivet.

The whisky has a world reputation for its full flavour which was established as far back as a century ago. It is light to medium in weight, has a trace of sweetness and is very palatable.

Glenfarclas Distillery was founded in 1836 by a farmer who sold out to John Grant in 1865 for £511. It is still owned by the Grant family, a connection which spans two centuries and five generations. The old maltings were closed in 1972, though little else has been changed. The stills are exactly the same shape as the original ones. The visitor centre, which offers free drams, is furnished with panelling from the ocean liner *Australia*. The centre has a reconstructed whisky bothy and an illicit still. The product is widely prized for blending. The eight-year-old 105° proof is the strongest malt whisky on the market.

A little farther north is Tamdhu distillery. It was built on the banks of the Spey in 1896 by a group of blenders; in 1975 the distillery was completely rebuilt. The visitor centre is the former disused railway station of Knockando, giving the building a chance to interest bothy whisky enthusiasts and railway buffs. The product is of medium weight, with a sweetish aroma, and leaves the palate with a satisfying mellow finish to the dram.

The last distillery on the Whisky Trail is Glen Grant, in the village of Rothes. Built in 1840, it was for nearly forty years the only distillery in Rothes until it was joined by three others in 1878-9. The water is taken from the Glen Grant Burn which rushes down from the hills to the west through a ravine. The product has always been high on the list of whisky connoisseurs who have valued its availability at various proofs and ages. It has a light aroma in its earlier years; the later age bottlings offer a fine rounded taste to the palate which is reminiscent of some fine French brandies.

The Whisky Trail covers a distance of some 60 miles and takes from four to six hours to cover, assuming one stops at each distillery. Leave time to linger!

It should be said that a number of other distilleries in the Speyside area extend a welcome to visitors, provided one contacts the local tourist office to ascertain whether a guided tour can be accommodated. Some have limited facilities for visitors while others are developing their facilities. One alternative to the whisky trail is the Cairngorm Whisky Centre and Museum at Inverdruie, near Aviemore. Here one can view many whisky relics and enjoy the facilities of the tasting room where one can sample the products of over 70 distilleries. There is an audio-visual presentation about distilling and its history.

APPENDIX I

The Speyside Way

The Speyside Way is only the second long-distance footpath to have been officially designated by the Countryside Commission for Scotland. When completed, this footpath will run for some 60 miles between Tugnet, at the mouth of the Spey, to Glenmore Lodge at Aviemore. The Way is still under development and at present only the northern section has been routed and signposted. This part goes from Tugnet to Ballindalloch. It stretches for 30 miles and was opened in 1981.

The purpose of the long-distance footpaths is to provide walkers and others with access to those parts of the countryside not available to those with cars. In this context these Ways (the other is the West Highland Way running from Milngavie, just north of Glasgow, to Fort William) offer the chance to travel unimpeded through a variety of scenic vistas.

The Speyside Way begins at Tugnet, on the Spey Estuary, which has long been famed for its salmon-netting activity. The Spey, in fact, is among the very best salmon rivers in Scotland. Running in from north Atlantic waters, the mature fish make for the ancestral home with an uncanny instinct: to the tributaries of the Spey and the source of the Spey itself, in Loch Spey, where the fish were originally spawned.

At the height of the fishing season, some 30 men are employed by the River Spey Commercial Fishery, operated by the Crown Estates since 1937. The fish are netted, caught and then prepared for export to southern markets packed in ice. The Ice House at Tugnet has a permanent exhibition telling the story of the salmon and the local industry on which it is based.

From Tugnet, the Speyside Way takes a pleasant and leisurely route to Spey Bay and then south across the now disused railway line which once connected all the towns on the Moray Firth coast. Skirting the western bounds of Gordon Castle estate, the path goes through Fochabers, past the tiny hamlet of Ordiequish to Boat of Brig. The walker is then taken through the Ardnilly estate to Craigellachie, with an optional detour to Dufftown. Still following the Spey, the path wends its way to Aberlour and through the crofting lands of Carron and Knockando. At Tamdhu the distillery there has converted the former railway station into an attractive visitors' centre devoted to the telling of the story of the alchemic conversion of barley and pure Highland water into liquid gold. There is a welcome opportunity for a tasting of malt whisky before making for Blacksboat and finally Ballindalloch near Bridge of Avon.

Following as it does the northern run to the Moray Firth of the Spey, the Speyside Way offers the walker a wide variety of scenery: from low-lying straths, through woodlands and low hills rising to the massifs of the Grampian Mountains. The long-standing human history of the Spey is never far away: only the shape of the settlements has changed.

As for wildlife, the Way offers a better chance than most to see Nature in the raw as it were. Roe deer, red deer, kestrels, ptarmigan, fox, red squirrel all tend to be less elusive, reflecting the fact that the human element is so unobtrusive. There is, too, ample opportunity to take one's time. On the Speyside Way there is no need to rush just 'to do' the Walk.

A Ranger Service operates on the Way to provide information and advice to users on the route. The Service is based at Craigellachie (tel: Craigellachie 266) if it is needed.

The development of the southern portion of the Speyside Way is still being considered by the Countryside Commission. The fact that the route is not quite open should not deter the walker who wishes to get to Aviemore. Judicious use of the OS maps will reveal walking paths which will keep one away from the main road traffic.

APPENDIX II

Walking the Hills – Precautions for Walkers

Despite the fact that many tens of thousands visit Speyside each year, there is still the opportunity of getting off the beaten track to find ample solitude in the forests, on the hills and on the mountains. The search for solitude, however, must be accompanied by caution, for even experienced hill-walkers at times find themselves in difficulties created by the fickle nature of the weather, particularly on the higher levels of the Cairngorms. The advice given here is not complete and the reader's attention is drawn to the short list of books at the end of this section.

It should be remembered that the features which make the Cairngorms so attractive are also those which can present difficulties. Nature is mistress in her environment and those who wish to meet her must go prepared. People have become lost, been injured and have died in the Cairngorms; not all of these have been ill-prepared.

Because the Cairngorms are so high there is every likelihood of mists, rain, snow, high winds and low temperatures being encountered. One can easily encounter the whole spectrum of a year's weather in one day on the hills and peaks. And although they are accessible, they can also be remote, so that one can find oneself up to ten miles from the nearest road or inhabited house, with the distance between help and safety covered by 'ups and downs' which are both tiring and strength-sapping.

Snow conditions are sometimes difficult to assess. Hard-packed snow on one side of a hill could turn to soft, deep powder on the other side which is difficult to traverse, even on skis. On exposed plateaux the wind can often whip up snow into drifts which can cover streams and burns with false bridges. Snow overhangs can present significant danger as can the build-up of snow on slopes which could avalanche.

Exposure is another danger, resulting from leaving a base with inadequate clothing and then encountering bad weather which leads to disorientation. At least fifty per cent of deaths on the Cairngorms have been the result of exposure, exhaustion and hypothermia.

This catalogue of dangers is meant to highlight the need for common sense. For instance, it is essential before any foray into the hills to leave at one's base information about the route being taken and the approximate time of return. Nearly three-quarters of fatalities have resulted from a party failing to turn back at the onset of bad weather or having decided to change from the planned route. A point to remember is that people have disappeared completely in the Cairngorms, their bodies being found months after the incident, or in some cases, never at all.

Mountain Rescue Teams are on call in the area:

Aviemore Police Station (Aviemore 222 or 380)

Glenmore Lodge (Cairngorm 256)

White Lady Shieling, Cairngorm (Cairngorm 230)

These rescue services are different from the ski rescue services which operate during the winter at Cairngorm, and then only on the heavily used piste areas.

It is useful to remember that even if one meets very few other people on walks or rambles, the environment is being shared. Many people are in fact encountered who have a specific relationship with land: landowners, workers, the Forestry Commission, Countryside Rangers, the National Trust, farmers and other users.

In Scotland there is no law of trespass. However, when going on to privately owned land it is courtesy to ask permission from the owners, except where a public Right of Way exists. There are occasions and certain times of the year when permission can be refused and one may be asked to leave. In the lambing season (from March to May) and in the stalking and shooting season (usually August to October) restrictions are usually placed on access to land. Local enquiries can usually reveal the times when access is denied.

There are a few basic rules to be observed when using the countryside:

Keep to paths when going over estates and farmland.

Observe any restrictions advised by landowners.

Do not leave litter lying about.

Keep dogs under control and preferably on a leash.
In forests, keep to the paths and do not light fires.
Safeguard water supplies.
Protect wildlife and plants.
Close all gates.

For those who intend going on to higher levels of ground, there are again a few basic rules to be observed, all to do with one's safety:

Be properly equipped, including good walking boots, warm clothing, spare clothing, a map, compass, torch, whistle, first aid, spare food and a polythene bag.

Plan ahead with a calculation of the time taken to complete the route. Record this on a Route Card, with bad weather alternatives, and hand it to someone responsible. Always report your return.

Familiarise yourself with local rescue facilities, telephone numbers and the location of shelter bothies.

Confident and accurate map and compass work is a fundamental in hill safety. The green-backed OS maps with a scale of 1:25,000 (about 2.5 inches to the mile) are excellent for precise details of ground conditions. They, however, cover only small areas of the countryside. The special OS Outdoor Leisure map on 'The High Tops' (Cairngorms) is also on the 1:25,000 scale but covers much of the area in a complete section. Most of the green maps cover the hill ground in the area: but maps for some of the lower hills have yet to be published. Always use the newer metric scale maps, which have greater detail than the older maps which used the inch scales.

Never allow your party to split up.

Always observe weather forecasts and ensure that the local forecasting service is used.

Never go on winter expeditions unless backed up by experience. Arctic conditions prevail with all the attendant dangers of wind, snow, avalanche and whiteout.

Recognising the increased demand for walking in Strathspey, a number of books have been produced which recommend easy to moderate walks in a particular locality. The following are recommended:

Walks in the Cairngorms by E.L. Cross (Luath Press Ltd)

A Walker's Companion to the Wade Roads by Joan and Arthur Baker (Melven Press)

Footpath Map and Visitors' Guide by the Rothiemurchus Estate Office

Walks around Tomintoul (Tourist Office, Tomintoul)

Local Walks around Newtonmore (Tourist Office, Newtonmore)

Other books recommended include:

Mountain Craft and Leadership by E. Langmuir (Mountain Leadership Training Boards of Great Britain)

Police Mountain Codes

The Cairngorms by Adam Watson (Scottish Mountaineering Club)

Climbers' Guide to the Cairngorms (Scottish Mountaineering Club)

Heading for the Scottish Hills (Scottish Mountaineering Club)

APPENDIX III

The 'Spey' Name

The derivation of the name 'Spey' is rather obscure. The most acceptable meaning is from the Gaelic word 'speidh', meaning rapidity or strength, certainly two characteristics of the river. One authority has suggested that the name is derived from the Teutonic 'spe' (sputum) 'because the rapidity of it raiseth much foam and froth'. On an ancient map drawn by Ptolemy, AD 150, the river is shown flowing into *Tuessis Aestuarium*. A later map of the fourteenth century, made by Richard of Cirencester, shows the Spey with the name of *Tuessis;* a Roman station about thirty miles from the river mouth bears the same name as the river, which is depicted as flowing into *Tuessis Aestuarium*. There is a tradition that the Spey had its outflow into the Moray Firth some three miles west of Kingston, the argument being based on the presence of a small cairn known locally as Spey's Law. But there seems to be no physical evidence to suggest that this was ever the case.

That the mouth of the river was a mile west of its present position is suggested in a paper in the *Journal of the Royal Scottish Geographical Society:* 'So far no good evidence has been found to support the old tradition that the Spey once ran westward in a narrow cut parallel to the shore, and entered the sea three miles distant from its present mouth and opposite to a hill (*sic*) called Spey's Law. Many centuries ago it may have entered the sea about a mile west of the present mouth where air photographs show that the shingle forms a number of hooks curving into a strip of low-lying ground, marked as a morass in McGill's map of 1725'.

Locally this morass is known as The Streeds, and there is strong evidence that it marks an ancient bed of the Spey.

Index